EVERYTHING I KNOW

ABOUT COOKING

I learned from the

COUNTRY WOMEN'S ASSOCIATION OF NSW

murdoch books

Sydney | London

CONTENTS

INTRODUCTION

Few organisations can boast a history that goes back almost a century, but the Country Women's Association of New South Wales has succeeded where so many others have failed: it's recognised the need to evolve in line with changing community – and member – expectations, while remaining true to the core values on which it was established.

The CWA of NSW was formed in 1922 at a time when country women were fighting isolation and a lack of health facilities. The branches that were established became a friendship group for members, but they also became so much more. They threw their efforts and resources behind setting up baby health care centres, funding bush nurses and building and staffing maternity wards, hospitals, schools and rest homes.

In the decades that followed, the CWA of NSW became an influential voice for country communities, turning its attention to advocacy around the issues of the day and lobbying government departments and representatives. Today, that focus remains unchanged, and the CWA is recognised as one of the most powerful lobby groups in the nation, particularly for rural and regional Australia.

Some people still think primarily of cooking and craft when it comes to the CWA. These skills continue to hold an important place within the organisation. Members are also speaking up on behalf of their communities, and their ranks are continuing to grow.

The CWA of NSW is evolving to work in new environments, but still under the same banner of improving conditions and life for women, children and families.

For more information, see our website www.cwaofnsw.org.au or telephone 02 8337 0200.

CATERING HINTS

Although some caterers have different ideas on quantities, these quantities are tried, tested and treasured. We hope this information prevents over-catering, or even worse, preparing too little.

TEA 30 g for 6; 250 g for 50 (30 g equals about 7 teaspoons). For tea or coffee, use 2 litres for 40 people.

INSTANT COFFEE 125 g makes 50 small cups; 500 g coffee makes 250 white or 130–150 black coffees.

SUGAR 500 g sugar serves 50; 500 g loaf sugar equals approximately 112 blocks.

BUTTER 250 g butter per 1 kg loaf of bread; or combine 175 g creamed butter and 60 ml warm milk per 1 kg loaf of bread, which is more economical and easier to spread.

BREAD 680 g loaf makes 10 sandwiches or 25 slices to one loaf; 750 g loaf equals 12 double slices; 1 kg loaf equals 16 double slices; and 16 double slices cut in quarters serve 20 people. **Egg filling for sandwiches**: 6–8 hard-boiled eggs, mashed with butter and salt and pepper, per 1 kg loaf.

SOUP 8 litres serves 50 people, based on ¾–1 cup per person.

CHEESE 1 kg serves 50.

SALAD 6 large lettuces, shredded, serve 50; 1.25 kg tomatoes, thinly sliced, serve 50.

MEAT AND POULTRY 60–90 g cooked boned meat or poultry per person; 325 g per person for uncooked meat cuts off the bone. **Boneless cuts or sausages** up to 250 g each; **Chicken** 1.5 kg serves 6–8; one size 18 chicken serves 4 people; 9 kg chicken thighs equals about 70 pieces. **Ham** 7 medium tomatoes to 1 kg. **Sandwich meat** 50–300 g chopped or minced meat or chicken per 1 kg loaf. **Turkey** 9 kg serves 25 people.

CASSEROLE Serves 6–8.

RICE 500 g uncooked rice serves 16 when cooked; 1 cup uncooked rice yields 3 cups cooked rice.

VEGETABLES **Beetroot** 25 slices per 825 g can or 100 slices per 3 kg can. **Carrots** 1 kg, cut into rings, serves 20. **Peas** 2 kg frozen peas serves 30–35. **Potatoes** 3.25 kg cooked potato with extras serves 50; 3 kg potato (mashed) equals 30 good servings.

CAKES AND DESSERTS
Cheesecake or tart 23 cm tart cuts into 10–12 pieces (1 serve per person). **Custard** 4.5 litres serves 50. **Fruit salad** One 900 g can serves 10–12 (½ cup each). **Ice-cream** 1 litre serves 8–10; 4 litres yields 35 scoops. **Pavlova** (based on 4 eggs) serves 10–12. **Small cakes and slices** provide 2 per person or 3 each for two people. **Sponges** (deep 20 cm round sponges): cut a small circle in the centre and cut into 10 slices.

EXHIBITION TIPS

BISCUITS

Keep within the class named. Do not use too much shortening as biscuits become greasy; use about half as much fat as flour. A mixture of self-raising flour with plain flour or cornflour gives the best results. Roll thinly and cut into dainty shapes or use a biscuit forcer, as this attracts more credit than drop biscuits. Bake slowly to prevent breakage and loss of shape. To present correctly, arrange a few biscuits of each variety, whether plain or fancy, on a plate, unless a box of biscuits is stated. Biscuits can be stored for a week in an airtight container.

BUTTER CAKES

Use butter or first-grade table margarine. All ingredients should be at room temperature, or slightly warm butter, milk and eggs in hot water. For the quick-mix method, butter should be very soft, but not melted. If an electric mixer is used, beat in flour on speed 2 for up to 2 minutes. When mixing, add flour and milk alternately, beginning and ending with flour. Vigorously beat flour that contains gluten; this will result in a fine texture. Before placing in an oven, make a graduated hollow in the centre of large cakes, to assist even rising. Use a moderate oven, as a hot oven seizes the sides, causing the cake to set too soon, dome and crack. A cake with a small crack, that is otherwise good, is better than a smooth-topped one which is sodden inside. Cool cake in pan for up to 15 minutes before turning out. A rainbow cake is a butter cake and must be layered from the base in the order of chocolate, pink and white. Butter cakes cut better when 1 day old.

CHOCOLATE CAKES

This should be a block cake, light but not crumbly, and even in texture and in colour (dark reddish-brown) on the base and sides. It should not have large holes or wet streaks. Flavouring must be chocolate with no trace of excess soda. Cracks are disregarded, if cake is otherwise good. Use any shape pan. A layer cake with cream is not a chocolate cake. Chocolate cake may be iced with chocolate icing and decorated simply.

DARK FRUIT CAKES

Some competitions specify a 20 cm size pan. If no size is given, a very large cake does not gain more points than a smaller one. Cake should be smooth on top, well risen, but not domed. A slight crack is not a defect. Should be firm with more fruit than cake, but not dry. Fruit should be evenly distributed. Cake is best if cut up before serving. It should not have damp patches, sodden streaks or holes. The flavour should be a rich fruit, without too much spice. The cake needs approximately 3 weeks to mature; a light fruit cake can be made 2–3 days early. Stand the cake in the tin until cold, to avoid breaking.

LAMINGTONS

Judges should state their preferred size; most prefer lamingtons not higher than 3.7 cm, but some allow 4.5 cm. Should be a butter cake mixture. Texture should be fine and moist. Leave cake until the next day before cutting. Icing should be even and well flavoured, and the coconut should be fresh, not soaked or covered in chocolate. When cut, coating should not have soaked into the cake.

SCONES

Present no more than 6 unbuttered scones. Shortening should be one-tenth the weight of flour; too much makes scones crisp. Avoid too much liquid and too much handling. Glaze tops with milk, or milk and egg. Very large scones are not as attractive as smaller ones, and round scones are preferred to other shapes. Use a 2.5 cm deep tin and stand scones close together, to retain steam and soften scones. Remove from oven and wrap in a clean towel. Remove excess flour or grease from scone base. Bake and cool just before exhibition. Break scones open, never cut them.

SPONGES

Use fresh eggs. A temperature of 21°C gives best results. The cake should be made just long enough to cool before exhibition. Layers should be even in height (weigh empty pans, then weigh again when filled with mixture) with no overhanging edges or tucks. The top should be smooth, not sticky, and without sugar or soda spots, or crack marks. Some judges allow a fine sprinkling of icing sugar, but most prefer a plain top. Grease and flour tin, then shake off excess flour. Mix beaten eggs and caster sugar until sugar dissolves, as the texture of the sponge is thus determined. Sift flour at least three times, to incorporate as much air as possible. Make sure liquid is well blended in the mixture, or the top of the cake will be streaky. Do not place the scraping from the bowl in the centre of the layer, as this could show when cut. Divide mixture between two tins. When cooked, allow cake to stand in tin for a few minutes before turning out. Turn out onto a clean folded tea-towel, then turn right side up. If top remains on the tea-towel, the cake has a moist surface. If turned onto a wire rack, the wire would mark the top of the cake.

SULTANA CAKES

The crust should be a lighter brown than that of a fruit cake. Colour and fruit distribution should be even. There should be more cake than fruit. Do not use spices. If lemon essence is used, it should not be too strong.

MEASURING UP

OVEN TEMPERATURES

	Celsius	Fahrenheit	Gas mark
Very slow	120	250	1
Slow	150	300	2
Moderately slow	160	325	3
Moderate	180–190	350–375	4
Moderately hot	200–210	400–425	5
Hot	220–230	450–475	6
Very hot	240–250	500–525	7

DRY MEASURES   LIQUID MEASURES

Metric	Imperial	Metric	Imperial
30 g	1 oz	30 ml	1 fluid oz
60 g	2 oz	60 ml	2 fluid oz
90 g	3 oz	100 ml	3 fluid oz
155 g	5 oz	150 ml	5 fluid oz (¼ pint)
250 g	8 oz (½ lb)	250 ml	8 fluid oz
500 g	16 oz (1 lb)	500 ml	16 fluid oz
1 kg	32 oz (2 lb)	1000 ml (1 litre)	1¾ pints

CHAPTER ONE

EVERYTHING I KNOW

ABOUT MAKING

SNACKS, SOUPS AND SANDWICHES

MARINATED CHICKEN WINGS

1.5 kg chicken wings
¼ cup soy sauce
1 clove garlic or 1 teaspoon crushed garlic
2 tablespoons dry sherry
1 teaspoon grated ginger
2 teaspoons brown sugar
1 tablespoon honey
Salt and pepper

Separate chicken wings at the joints into three pieces and discard the tips. Mix remaining ingredients together and combine with chicken in a bowl. Cover and refrigerate overnight, stirring once or twice. Pour chicken and marinade into a baking dish. Bake in a moderate oven for 35–40 minutes. Serve hot or cold as an appetiser.

CHILLI NUTS

2–3 tablespoons oil
6 large pappadams, broken into pieces
2 cups Rice Bubbles
2 cups sultanas
250 g salted cashews
250 g salted peanuts
Pinch chilli powder, or to taste

Heat oil in pan. Add pappadam pieces, stirring until cooked and puffed. Add Rice Bubbles and cook for 1 minute. Stir in sultanas, cashews and peanuts. Cook for 2 minutes, stirring constantly. Remove from heat, then stir in chilli powder. Cool. Store in an airtight container. Makes 10 cups.

SPANISH TORTILLA

½ cup olive oil
2 large all-purpose potatoes, cut into 5 mm slices
2 large onions, sliced
3 eggs
Salt and pepper

Heat the oil in a 20 cm diameter deep non-stick frying pan with a lid. Place alternate layers of potato and onion in the pan, cover and cook for 8 minutes over low heat. Using tongs, turn the layers in sections (it doesn't matter if the layers break up). Cover and cook for a further 8 minutes, without allowing the potato to colour.

Put a strainer over a bowl and drain the potato mixture, reserving 1 tablespoon of the oil.

Put the eggs and a little salt and pepper in a bowl and whisk to combine. Add the potato mixture, pressing down with the back of a spoon to completely cover with the egg.

Heat the reserved oil in the same frying pan over high heat. Pour in the egg mixture, pressing down to even it out. Reduce the heat to low, cover with a lid and cook for 12 minutes, or until set. Gently shake the pan to ensure the tortilla is not sticking. Leave to cook for 5 minutes, then invert onto a plate. Cut into wedges. Serve tortilla at room temperature.

SAVOURY CAKES

1 egg
1 cup milk
½ cup self-raising flour
1 cup grated cheese
100 g chopped bacon
1 tablespoon chopped parsley

Beat egg and add to milk. In another bowl, sift flour, then add the cheese, bacon and parsley. Pour in milk and egg and mix well. Place dessertspoonfuls into greased mini muffin tins. Bake in a moderate oven for 15 minutes. Makes 24.

SAVOURY STICKS

2 sheets frozen puff pastry, thawed
1 egg, beaten
Sundried tomato paste or olive paste
Grated parmesan cheese
Cayenne pepper (optional)
Poppy or sesame seeds
Grated tasty cheese, extra

Cut each sheet of pastry in half and brush with egg. Spread one side of the pastry with a filling based on sun-dried tomato paste or olive paste and parmesan cheese. Sprinkle with cayenne pepper. Press the two sides of the pastry together firmly with a rolling pin. Cut into strips about 1 cm wide. Twist strips into loose corkscrews and place on a baking tray. Brush with more egg. Sprinkle with poppy seeds or sesame seeds. Bake in a hot oven until golden brown (about 10 minutes), adding extra cheese when almost ready.

SEAFOOD PÂTÉ

250 g smoked salmon or hot smoked trout or mackerel
250 g cream cheese
1 tablespoon lemon juice
1 tablespoon grated onion
1 tablespoon tomato sauce or 3 tablespoons mayonnaise
¼ teaspoon Worcestershire sauce

Finely chop the fish or mince it in a blender. If using a blender, add remaining ingredients and blend again. Alternatively, place remaining ingredients in a bowl and thoroughly mix, then mix in fish. Place in a 500 ml container or shape as desired. Chill. Serve with crackers or as a spread.

CORN FRITTERS

60 g butter
½ cup plain flour
2 eggs, lightly beaten
¼ cup tinned creamed corn
Salt and pepper
1 tablespoon grated parmesan cheese
Oil, for deep-frying

Combine butter with ½ cup water in a small pan and stir until butter has melted. Bring to boil, then remove from the heat. Stir in the flour. Return pan to heat and stir until mixture leaves the sides of the pan. Transfer to a mixing bowl. Cool slightly, then gradually add the beaten eggs. Beat with electric mixers until mixture is smooth, thick and shiny. Beat in the creamed corn, salt, pepper and cheese. Making only two or three fritters at a time, drop level tablespoons of the mixture into moderately hot oil. Cook until golden and doubled in size. Remove and drain on paper towel.

SAUSAGE ROLLS

3 sheets frozen puff pastry, thawed
2 eggs, lightly beaten
750 g sausage mince
1 onion, finely chopped
1 garlic clove, crushed
1 cup fresh breadcrumbs
3 tablespoons chopped flat-leaf (Italian) parsley
3 tablespoons chopped thyme
½ teaspoon ground sage
½ teaspoon freshly grated nutmeg
½ teaspoon ground cloves
½ teaspoon pepper

Preheat the oven to 200°C. Lightly grease two baking trays.

Cut the pastry sheets in half and lightly brush the edges with some of the beaten egg.

Mix half the remaining egg with the remaining ingredients in a large bowl, then divide into six even portions. Pipe or spoon filling down the centre of each piece of pastry, then brush edges with some of the egg. Fold the pastry over the filling, overlapping the edges and placing the join underneath. Brush the rolls with more egg, then cut each into six short pieces.

Cut two small slashes on top of each roll, place on the baking trays and bake for 15 minutes. Reduce the heat to 180°C and bake for another 15 minutes, or until puffed and golden.

CHEESE AND BACON STRAWS

1 teaspoon oil
4 bacon rashers, finely chopped
2 sheets ready-rolled puff pastry, thawed
1 egg, lightly beaten
1 cup grated tasty cheese
2 spring onions, chopped
1 tablespoon chopped parsley
1 teaspoon paprika

Heat oil in a pan. Add bacon and cook until crisp; leave to drain on absorbent paper.

Brush pastry sheets with a little egg, then sprinkle a quarter of the cheese over half of each sheet, leaving a 1 cm border. Sprinkle with combined bacon, spring onions, parsley, paprika and remaining cheese. Fold sheets in half to enclose filling. Press together lightly, then brush surface with a little more egg. Cut crossways into 1 cm strips. Twist strips, then place about 3 cm apart onto greased trays.

Bake at 200°C for about 12 minutes or until lightly browned; allow to cool on wire racks. Makes about 40.

GUACAMOLE

3 ripe avocados
1 tablespoon lime or lemon juice (see Hint)
1 tomato
1–2 red chillies, finely chopped
1 small red onion, finely chopped
1 tablespoon finely chopped coriander leaves
2 tablespoons sour cream
1–2 drops Tabasco sauce
Pepper
Corn chips, to serve

Roughly chop the avocado flesh and place in a bowl. Mash lightly with a fork and sprinkle with lemon juice to prevent the avocado from discolouring.

Cut the tomato in half horizontally and use a teaspoon to scoop out the seeds. Finely dice the flesh and add to the avocado.

Stir in the chilli, onion, coriander, sour cream and Tabasco sauce. Season with pepper.

Serve immediately or cover the surface with plastic wrap and refrigerate for 1–2 hours. If refrigerated, allow to come to room temperature before serving. Serve with corn chips.

HINT: You will need 1–2 limes to produce 1 tablespoon of juice, depending on the lime. A heavier lime will probably be juicier. To get more juice from a citrus fruit, prick it all over with a fork and then heat on high (100%) in the microwave for 1 minute. Don't forget to prick it or the fruit may burst.

CHICKEN STOCK

Chicken bones or trimmings
Lemon juice
Bay leaf
Black pepper

Combine all ingredients with 2 litres water and bring to the boil.
Simmer for 1 hour and strain. Remove bay leaf. Refrigerate or freeze.

SPRING CHICKEN SOUP

1 litre vegetable stock
2 tablespoons baby peas
40 g instant noodles
1 carrot, grated
1 spring onion, finely sliced
1 chicken breast, finely sliced
1 small teaspoon chicken stock powder
Pinch onion powder
Pinch celery powder
Pinch salt

Bring stock to the boil, then add peas and noodles. Re-boil stock,
then add carrot and onion. Simmer for 3–5 minutes. Add chicken,
chicken stock powder, onion powder, celery powder and salt, and
heat through. Serve in heated bowls with freshly baked scones.

GINGER CARROT SOUP

30 g butter or margarine
4 cups sliced carrots
1 large onion, chopped
2 teaspoons grated orange peel
1 teaspoon grated fresh ginger or
   ¼ teaspoon ground ginger
3 cups chicken stock
½ cup milk
1 or 2 tablespoons orange juice
Salt and pepper
Thin orange or lemon slices, or parsley, to garnish

Melt butter in a saucepan over a low heat. Add carrots, onion, orange peel and ginger and cook gently for 5 minutes, stirring occasionally. Add stock and heat mixture until it boils. Reduce heat immediately, cover and simmer for 10 minutes. Purée mixture in batches in a blender until smooth. Return to saucepan, stir in milk, then orange juice. Heat gently to serving temperature. Season to taste, garnish and serve.

NAMEKO (JAPANESE GOLDEN MUSHROOM SOY SOUP)

100 g soy paste
1 teaspoon mirin wine
1½ cups dashi
100 g nameko (golden mushrooms)
250 g tofu, diced
1 shallot stalk, chopped

Combine soy paste, mirin and dashi in a saucepan and heat gently
to make soy soup. Divide the nameko and the diced tofu into soup
bowls. Using a ladle, pour hot soy soup over the nameko and tofu.
Sprinkle chopped shallots over each bowl as a garnish. This soup can
also be served after the main meal, as it cleanses the palate. Serves 5.

GOULASH SOUP

1 heaped teaspoon lard or oil
400 g beef shin or rump, cut into 2 cm cubes
2 chopped onions
1 heaped teaspoon hot paprika
1 level teaspoon salt
400 g potatoes, diced

Melt lard or heat oil in a saucepan and gently sauté beef and onion.
When onion is transparent, add the paprika, stir, then pour in 2 litres
water. Bring to the boil then add salt. Lower heat, cover the pan and
simmer for 1½ hours or until meat is almost tender. Add potatoes
and cook until both meat and potatoes are tender.

HUNGARIAN GOULASH SOUP

1 tablespoon lard or oil
2 onions, chopped
½ teaspoon ground caraway seeds (optional)
400 g beef shin or rump, diced
1 carrot, sliced
2 green or red capsicums, sliced
1 tomato, peeled and chopped
1 parsley root or parsnip
1 clove garlic, crushed
1 teaspoon medium hot or hot paprika
500 g potatoes, diced
Salt

CSIPETKE (PINCHED DOUGH)
1 egg
5 heaped tablespoons plain flour

Melt the lard or heat the oil in a pan and fry onion gently until golden. Sprinkle with caraway seeds. Add meat, carrot, capsicums, tomato, parsley root, garlic and paprika. Cover pan and leave to simmer. As juices evaporate, gradually add about 2 litres of water to achieve desired consistency. After about 2 hours, add potatoes and bring to the boil. Add salt to taste. Make the csipetke (see below) and add to soup.

To make csipetke, beat egg and mix with sifted flour to make a stiff dough. Roll or pull small pieces of dough (about the size of a hazelnut) from the mixture and drop them into boiling soup about 5 minutes before soup is ready. When the csipetke rise to the surface, the goulash is ready to serve.

PEA AND HAM SOUP

2 cups dried split peas (see Note)
1 kg ham shanks or bones
2 onions, minced or finely chopped
2 bay leaves
Salt and pepper, to taste
2 cups milk
2 tablespoons flour, sifted

Wash peas and soak in 1.5 litres water overnight. Place ham, peas, water in which peas were soaked, onions, bay leaves, and salt and pepper in a pressure cooker. Cover with lid and pressure cook for 20 minutes. Allow cooker to cool slowly. Add milk to flour and beat until smooth before adding to soup. Cook uncovered for 2–3 minutes until thickened.

NOTE: This soup can be made satisfactorily without soaking peas, if 15 minutes more cooking time in the pressure cooker is allowed.

PUMPKIN SOUP

2 medium onions, diced
4 bacon rashers, diced
1 clove garlic, crushed
3 cups diced pumpkin
1 tablespoon tomato paste
3 cups chicken stock
1 bay leaf
Salt and pepper, to taste
Pinch cayenne pepper
½ cup evaporated milk

Fry onions and bacon in oil. Add garlic, pumpkin, tomato paste and stock. Bring to the boil, adding bay leaf, salt, pepper and cayenne. Cover and simmer for 25 minutes. Remove from heat and allow to cool. Remove bay leaf and put mixture through blender. Return to saucepan, add evaporated milk and heat slowly.

PUMPKIN AND LENTIL SOUP

500 g peeled and diced pumpkin
¾ cup dried red lentils
2 teaspoons chicken stock powder
1 teaspoon ground cumin
4 lean bacon rashers, finely chopped
Parsley, to garnish

Place all ingredients except the bacon and parsley in a large saucepan along with 1.5 litres of water. Bring to the boil, then simmer for 45 minutes, skimming when necessary. Allow to stand and cool. Purée and add more water or stock for the desired consistency. Cook bacon until crisp. Sprinkle bacon and parsley over soup and serve. Serves 4–6.

PUMPKIN AND ORANGE SOUP

30 g butter
1 medium onion, chopped
1–2 tablespoons freshly grated ginger
1.5 kg pumpkin, unpeeled
Grated zest and juice of 1 large orange
1.5 litres chicken stock
Salt and pepper, to taste
Cream (optional)
Nutmeg
Pumpkin seeds, toasted (see Note)

Melt butter in a large pan and sauté the onion and ginger until soft. Peel pumpkin and cut into chunks, reserving the seeds. Place pumpkin in the pan with orange zest, juice and chicken stock. Bring to the boil, cover and simmer gently until pumpkin is cooked (about 20 minutes). Purée in batches in a blender or food processor and return to pan. Season to taste. Return to the boil. Divide among bowls, garnish with a swirl of cream. Sprinkle with fresh nutmeg and toasted pumpkin seeds and serve.

NOTE: To toast pumpkin seeds, rinse well, removing excess pulp. Place on a baking sheet and toast in a moderate oven for 20 minutes. Add a little salt. These also make a tasty snack on their own. Serves 6.

ZUCCHINI SOUP

50 g butter or margarine
1 kg zucchini, coarsely chopped
2 or 3 sticks celery, diced
2 medium brown onions, chopped finely
2 medium potatoes, coarsely chopped
3 carrots, finely chopped
1 teaspoon salt, or to taste
Pepper
1 small garlic clove, crushed (optional)
4 cups chicken stock
1 teaspoon fresh or dried tarragon leaves
Cream, to serve
Chopped parsley, to serve

Melt butter or margarine in a large saucepan. Add vegetables and toss until well coated. Cook for 5 minutes on low heat with the lid on, but do not allow to brown. Add salt, plenty of pepper and the crushed garlic if using. Pour in the chicken stock and the dried tarragon, if using. Simmer for approximately 15 minutes, or until vegetables are softened.

Put all ingredients through a blender, return to saucepan and add the fresh tarragon, if using. Heat soup and serve with a small dollop of cream in centre and sprinkled with chopped parsley.

This recipe is ideal for using up the excess from a crop of home-grown zucchini.

CHICKEN, ROCKET AND WALNUT SANDWICHES

2 tablespoons oil
250 g chicken breast
500 g chicken thigh
250 g whole-egg mayonnaise
100 g celery, finely chopped
90 g chopped walnuts
Salt and pepper
20 slices bread
1 large handful rocket

Heat the oil in a frying pan over medium heat and cook the chicken breast and thigh until lightly browned. Allow to cool, then finely chop the chicken.

Combine chicken with mayonnaise, celery and walnuts. Season to taste.

Make sandwiches using the chicken mixture and add the rocket to each. Remove the crusts and cut each sandwich into three fingers. Makes 30.

SMOKED SALMON AND CAPER BRUSCHETTA

1 baguette or crusty Italian loaf
Olive oil, for brushing
250 g cream cheese
2 tablespoons lemon juice
15 g snipped chives
100 g smoked salmon, sliced
2 tablespoons baby capers, rinsed
2 dill sprigs, to garnish

Cut the bread into 1 cm slices, brush with olive oil and grill until golden on both sides.

Mix the cream cheese with the lemon juice and chives. Spread over the toast and top with small slices of smoked salmon and a few baby capers. Garnish with sprigs of dill before serving. Makes about 24.

Salted capers have a better flavour and texture than those preserved in brine. Rinse them before using.

CHAPTER TWO

EVERYTHING I KNOW

ABOUT MAKING

MAIN DISHES

HELEN'S QUICK SPINACH QUICHE

2 tablespoons butter
1 small bunch spinach, chopped
1 onion, chopped
2 rashers bacon
1 cup grated tasty cheese
2 eggs
2 tablespoons plain flour, sifted
2 cups milk

Melt butter in a frying pan and fry spinach and onion. Grill bacon. Sprinkle cheese on the bottom of a greased medium quiche dish. Top with spinach, onion and chopped bacon. Beat eggs with flour and milk. Pour over spinach mixture and bake in a moderate oven for 40 minutes.

SAVOURY PIE

4 eggs
2 cups milk (or 1 cup cream and 1 cup milk)
½ cup self-raising flour, sifted
1 onion, finely chopped
¼ cup chopped parsley
200 g tin tuna or salmon, drained
½ cup grated tasty cheese
Pepper to taste

In a large bowl beat together eggs, milk and flour. Stir in remaining ingredients. Pour into a well-greased 30 cm pie dish and bake in moderate oven for 35–40 minutes or until top is browned. Serve hot or cold.

SWISS QUICHE

PASTRY
1⅓ cups plain flour
Pinch salt
Pinch paprika
250 g butter
125 g grated cheese
1 egg yolk, slightly beaten

FILLING
340 g tin asparagus cuts, drained, or 250 g fresh asparagus,
    lightly cooked and cut into lengths
125 g chopped ham (see Note)
4 eggs
1 tablespoon plain flour
¼ teaspoon salt
Pinch paprika
½ cup milk
1 cup sour cream
125 g grated cheese (optional)

To make pastry, sift flour, salt and paprika, rub in butter, add grated
cheese (100 g gruyère and 25 g parmesan makes a good blend) and
mix in egg yolk to make a dry dough. Roll out. Use to line a greased
20 cm quiche pan.

To make filling, arrange asparagus with ham in the pastry shell.
In a separate bowl, beat eggs, then add flour. Add salt, paprika,
milk and sour cream. Mix well. Pour over asparagus and ham, then
sprinkle with extra grated cheese, if desired (again 100 g gruyère
and 25 g parmesan). Bake in a hot oven for 10 minutes, then reduce
to moderate for 30–40 minutes.

NOTE: The ham may be replaced with the same quantity of prawns.

TUNA AND SILVERBEET QUICHE

4 large leaves silverbeet, core removed
2 leeks or 1 onion, chopped
1 sheet frozen shortcrust pastry, thawed, or
    a purchased frozen shortcrust pie case
2 large eggs
½ cup cream or milk
Salt and pepper
95 g tin tuna, drained
1 cup grated cheese
Grated cheese, extra

Wash silverbeet and chop well, adding some of the white stalks. Boil together with leeks in a little water for 5 minutes. Drain well and allow to cool. Grease a pie dish, line with pastry and bake in a moderate oven for 15 minutes. Beat eggs and cream with salt and pepper, then add tuna, cheese and silverbeet. Fill pastry case and top with more grated cheese. Bake in a moderate oven for 15 minutes or until set.

SPINACH QUICHE

3 eggs
1½ cups milk
1 cup grated cheese
1 small onion, diced
30 g butter, melted
½ cup self-raising flour, sifted
1 cup cooked spinach
Salt and pepper, to taste

Place all ingredients in a bowl and mix until well combined. Grease a 23 cm pie dish. Pour in mixture and bake in a moderate oven for approximately 1 hour.

ZUCCHINI SLICE

3 bacon rashers or 4 slices ham
375 g grated unpeeled zucchini
1 large onion, finely chopped
1 cup grated cheddar cheese
1 cup self-raising flour, sifted
½ cup oil
5 eggs
Salt and pepper

Remove rind from bacon and chop finely. Combine zucchini, onion, bacon, cheese, flour, oil and lightly beaten eggs. Season with salt and pepper. Pour into a well-greased 20 x 30 cm lamington pan and bake in a 180°C oven for 30–40 minutes or until browned. Serves 4–6.

IMPOSSIBLE PIE

¾ cup of pastry mix (if pastry mix is unavailable, use 125 g
   diced butter and ½ cup plain flour, rubbed in until well
   combined)
3 eggs
1 onion, chopped
1 small tin champignons, drained
2–3 rashers bacon, diced (pre-diced bacon may be used)
1 cup grated cheese
Salt and pepper
½ cup milk

Place the pastry mix (or the rubbed-in butter and flour) in a large bowl. Add remaining ingredients and combine well. Pour into a greased pie dish and bake at 180°C for 40–45 minutes.

VEGETABLE AND BACON QUICHE

BASE
4 tablespoons vegetable oil
4 tablespoons milk
1 cup self-raising flour

FILLING
1 medium grated carrot
1 medium zucchini
1 small onion
1 cup grated cheese
1 cup chopped bacon or ham (vegetarians can replace
    this with 1 cup grated pumpkin or a finely chopped
    tomato; see Note)
3 eggs
¾ cup milk
¾ cup self-raising flour
½ teaspoon salt and pinch of pepper

For the base, mix together oil and milk then stir into the flour. Press into the base and sides of a greased 23 x 4 cm quiche tin. Place quiche on an oven tray in case the filling overflows. Preheat oven to 180°C.

For the filling, combine vegetables, cheese and ham in a large bowl. In another bowl, combine the eggs, milk, flour, salt and pepper and add to the vegetables. Mix to combine. Pour into the prepared uncooked pastry base and bake for 40 minutes or until set.

Alternatively, place spoonfuls of base and filling mixture into a greased patty tin or mini muffin trays to make mini quiches. Bake 10–15 minutes for patty cases and 15–20 minutes for mini muffin tins. Makes eight good-sized meals served with vegetables or salads.

NOTE: If you have replaced the bacon with vegetables, the cooking time may need to be increased by 10–20 minutes.

TUNA, CORN AND ONION QUICHE

4 eggs
1 cup low-fat milk
½ cup buttermilk
Pepper
½ cup self-raising flour
125 g tin sweetcorn kernels, drained
4 green onions, sliced
425 g tin tuna chunks in brine, well drained and flaked
    (substitute 450 g tin red or pink salmon if preferred)
¾ cup low-fat grated tasty cheese
Baby rocket leaves and crusty bread, to serve

Preheat oven to 180°C. Lightly grease a 1.75 litre shallow quiche or baking dish. Whisk eggs, milk and buttermilk, season with pepper. Sift flour into bowl, stir through corn, onions, tuna and most of the cheese. Add egg mixture; mix well to combine. Pour into prepared dish, sprinkle with remaining cheese. Bake 35–40 minutes until set and golden. Cool slightly before cutting. Serve warm or cold with rocket and bread.

CHICKEN PIE

PASTRY
2 cups plain flour
½ teaspoon salt
140 g butter
1 teaspoon water

FILLING
Pinch of pepper
2 tablespoons plain flour
½ teaspoon ground nutmeg
1 kg chicken thigh fillets, trimmed and cut into 2.5 cm cubes
2 large leeks, chopped
1 onion, thinly sliced
200 g ham, cut into 1 cm strips
75 g butter, melted
½ cup chicken stock
1 egg, beaten, for glazing
½ cup cream

For the pastry, sift flour and salt into a bowl, rub in butter and add enough water to form a stiff dough. Knead lightly, then refrigerate. Preheat oven to 200°C. Grease a large shallow ovenproof dish with melted butter.

Combine pepper, flour and nutmeg in a plastic bag, toss chicken pieces in flour mixture until well coated. Shake off excess flour. Place half the leek and onion in layers over the base of prepared dish. Top with half the ham and chicken. Repeat layers using remaining onion, leek, ham and chicken. Drizzle melted butter over filling, add stock.

Roll pastry to fit dish. Glaze edges of dish with a little egg. Cover pie with pastry. Glaze with egg. Cut three deep slits in pastry for steam to escape — cream will be added through these later. Bake for 1 hour, or until pastry is golden brown and chicken is cooked. Remove from oven and leave to stand for 5 minutes. Pour cream into slits and allow to stand for 10 minutes before serving.

OVEN-FRIED MUSTARD CHICKEN

1½ tablespoons dijon mustard
1 tablespoon lemon juice
½ teaspoon crumbled dried rosemary
3 large cloves garlic, minced
Pinch of pepper
6 chicken thighs or breasts, skinned
3 cups cornflakes, crushed
6 tablespoons parmesan cheese

Heat oven to moderately hot. Combine mustard, lemon juice, rosemary, garlic and pepper, then use to coat chicken. Combine cornflakes and cheese in a bag; shake chicken pieces to coat with the crumb mixture. Grease a baking dish and arrange chicken pieces in a single layer. Sprinkle remaining crumbs on top. Cover with foil and bake for 20 minutes. Remove foil and bake until juices run clear when chicken is pricked with fork.

JUMBUCK STEW

2 tablespoons flour
1 teaspoon salt, or to taste
1 teaspoon pepper
1 teaspoon curry powder
¼ teaspoon ground ginger
1 kg lamb shoulder chops
2 tablespoons oil
1 large onion, sliced
1 tablespoon brown vinegar
2 tablespoons tomato sauce
2 tablespoons Worcestershire sauce
1 tablespoon brown sugar
½ cup stock
500 g pumpkin, peeled and cut into large chunks

Combine flour, salt, pepper, curry powder and ginger and use to coat trimmed chops. Heat half the oil in a heavy pan and brown chops on each side. Transfer to a plate. Add remaining oil and cook onion until soft. Return chops to pan. Mix vinegar, sauces, sugar and stock together and pour over chops. Cover, simmer, then reduce heat to low and simmer gently for 1 hour. Skim any fat from surface. Add pumpkin to pan. Cover and cook a further 30 minutes or until chops are tender. Serve with hot herbed damper with chopped fresh herbs or mixed dried herbs added to the dough. Serves 6.

MEATLOAF (MICROWAVE)

1 kg lean beef mince
1 onion, finely chopped
1½ cups wholemeal breadcrumbs
2 teaspoons mixed dried herbs
2 tablespoons tomato sauce
1 egg, beaten

Combine all ingredients. Press mixture into a 1.5 litre microwave loaf dish. Cook on medium–high for approximately 15 minutes. Rotate dish halfway through cooking. Stand, covered, for 5–10 minutes. The meat loaf is done when it has shrunk slightly from the sides of the dish and the centre is still moist. Drain off juices as they accumulate.

MEAT PATTIES (MICROWAVE)

500–600 g lean beef mince
½ onion, finely chopped
¾ cup wholemeal breadcrumbs
1 teaspoon mixed dried herbs
1 tablespoon tomato sauce
1 egg, beaten

Prepare patties or meatballs using half the ingredients of the Meatloaf recipe (see above). Preheat a browning dish on high for 6 minutes, then brush with oil. Quickly press both sides of patties firmly onto the base of dish. Cook on high, allowing approximately 1½ minutes per patty. Stand for 1–2 minutes.

ORIENTAL BEEF AND BEANS

500 g round steak
4 tablespoons oil
2 onions, cut into strips
250 g green beans, trimmed and cut into 5 cm pieces
1 cup sliced celery
½ cup sliced red and green capsicum
1½ tablespoons cornflour
1½ tablespoons soy sauce
1 cup beef stock
125 g fresh or 140 g tinned mushrooms, sliced

Trim fat from beef and slice steak finely into thin slices, 6–8 cm long. Heat oil in a frying pan and brown the steak quickly. Add onions, beans, celery and capsicum and cook for 5 minutes, stirring constantly. Blend cornflour with soy sauce and stock to make a smooth paste. Add mushrooms and paste to pan, stirring until the liquid is smooth. Reduce heat, cover pan and simmer until beans soften a little.

This dish is good served with Oriental
Ginger and Cashew Rice (see page 66).

PASTA WITH BACON, TOMATO AND OLIVES

2 onions, chopped
3 cloves garlic, chopped
3 bacon rashers, chopped
2 x 400 g tins tomatoes, chopped
2 teaspoons tomato paste
½ teaspoon mixed dried Italian herbs
½ teaspoon sugar
Black olives
Salt and pepper
500 g pasta
250 g mozzarella cheese
Tasty cheese, grated

Fry onion, garlic and bacon in a little oil until onion is soft. Add tomatoes, tomato paste, herbs, sugar and olives. Simmer for 10 minutes. Season with salt and pepper.

Cook pasta until tender. Place cooked pasta mixed with mozzarella in an ovenproof dish and cover with sauce. Top with grated tasty cheese and cook in a moderate oven until cheeses melt. Serve alone or with tossed salad and Italian bread.

POTATO MOUSSAKA

4 large potatoes
2 medium eggplants
Oil or butter, for frying
1 cup chopped onions
1 kg beef or lamb mince
2 cloves garlic
2 tablespoons Worcestershire sauce
800 g tin tomatoes, drained
2 tablespoons sugar

TOPPING
3 eggs
¾ cup grated tasty cheese
¾ cup parmesan cheese
1 cup cream

Slice potatoes and eggplants fairly thinly. Fry in oil or butter until lightly browned and set aside.

Sauté the chopped onions in a little butter, add meat, garlic and Worcestershire sauce and cook for 10 minutes, stirring often. Mash tomatoes with a fork and cook with sugar for 5 minutes, then combine with meat mixture. Grease a large casserole dish and line with some of the potato slices, cover with a layer of eggplant, then a layer of meat mixture, repeating layers until all mixture is used. Bake in a moderate oven for 45 minutes.

To make topping, beat eggs and combine cheeses and cream. Distribute over the moussaka and cook for a further 20 minutes until browned and firm.

STUFFED CHICKEN BREASTS

4 chicken breast fillets
4 thin slices ham
4 tablespoons grated cheese
4 large or 8 small asparagus spears
Plain flour
1 tablespoon oil
45 g butter
6 tablespoons Marsala
2 tablespoons chicken stock
Asparagus, extra, for garnishing

Flatten chicken between two pieces of plastic wrap, using a mallet or rolling pin. Place 1 slice of ham, 1 tablespoon of grated cheese and 1–2 asparagus spears on each chicken fillet. Roll up and secure with toothpicks. Roll in flour.

Heat oil and 30 g butter in a frying pan, add chicken rolls and cook until tender, turning frequently. Remove toothpicks and place in a serving dish; keep warm. Add remaining butter, Marsala and stock to the pan. Bring to boil then simmer for a few minutes, stirring all the time. Spoon over chicken rolls and garnish with the extra asparagus.

PASTIZZI

3 sheets ready-rolled puff pastry
400 g ricotta cheese
2 eggs
2 bacon rashers, chopped
½ cup frozen peas
Salt and pepper
Milk, to glaze

Thaw frozen pastry and cut into 23 cm squares. Dampen edges with water. With a fork, mix together remaining ingredients, except the milk. Place equal amounts of mixture in the centre of each square, raise corners of the pastry and seal edges to form a square envelope shape. Brush tops with milk. Bake at 180°C for 15–20 minutes until golden and crisp.

NORA'S FISH DISH (MICROWAVE)

1 large onion, sliced
1 tablespoon oil
Salt and pepper
1 tablespoon lemon juice
2 cups white sauce
500 g fish fillets
1 tablespoon chopped parsley
Breadcrumbs, for sprinkling
Parmesan cheese, for sprinkling

Cook onion in oil for 3 minutes. Add salt, pepper and lemon juice. Make a white sauce or use a prepared sauce mix and add to dish. Cut fish into pieces and cook separately for about 3 minutes on medium-high or until just cooked. Add to dish and stir in parsley. Sprinkle with breadcrumbs and cheese and heat through. Serves 4.

GREEK-STYLE ROAST CHICKEN

8 medium desiree potatoes, unpeeled
2 small brown onions or 1 large onion
1.4 kg free-range chicken
50 g butter, softened
3 garlic bulbs (1 bulb broken into cloves, and the
    other 2 bulbs peeled and roughly chopped)
8 sprigs thyme, roughly chopped
8 sprigs oregano, roughly chopped
1 lemon
200 ml extra virgin olive oil
Sea salt and pepper

Preheat oven to 240°C. Cook potatoes in a large pan of salted water for 25 minutes or until tender. Drain and set aside. Thickly slice the onions and place in base of a baking pan. Pat chicken dry with paper towel and trim wing tips. Slide fingertips underneath skin of breast and gently separate from flesh.

Mash together the butter, half of the chopped garlic and one third of the thyme and oregano. Push this mixture evenly under the skin of the chicken. Put one third of the remaining herbs and the remaining chopped garlic into the cavity. Halve the lemon and squeeze one half over the chicken. Put this squeezed lemon half into the chicken cavity. Slice the other lemon half into thin slices. Tuck a couple of slices between legs and breast, and put the rest over the chicken.

Put chicken in a baking dish. Scatter the unpeeled garlic cloves over chicken. Gently push down on potatoes with a masher and crush until skin splits. Arrange around chicken in baking dish. Drizzle chicken and potatoes with the olive oil and season with the salt and pepper. Scatter with the remaining herbs. Pour 50 ml water into dish and bake for 1 hour. Rest for 5–10 minutes. Serve with pan juices.

MAIN DISHES

MACARONI AND MINCE SLICE

MACARONI
1½ cups macaroni
30 g butter, melted
½ cup cream
2 eggs, lightly beaten
¾ cup grated tasty cheese
2 tablespoons grated parmesan cheese

MEAT SAUCE
60 g butter
1 clove garlic, crushed
1 onion, chopped
600 g beef mince
3 tablespoons tomato paste
2 teaspoons beef stock powder
Fresh parsley, to taste
Salt and pepper, to taste

CHEESE SAUCE
60 g butter
4 tablespoons plain flour
1½ cups milk
3 tablespoons grated tasty cheese
1 tablespoon chopped parsley
1 egg, lightly beaten

Cook the macaroni in a large saucepan of rapidly boiling water, uncovered, for 10 minutes or until just tender. Drain, then place in a 28 x 18 cm shallow ovenproof dish. Combine the remaining ingredients in a bowl and pour over macaroni.

For the meat sauce, heat the butter in a stainless steel or non-stick frying pan. Add the garlic and onion and cook, stirring, until onion is soft. Add mince and stir until well browned. Stir in the tomato paste, stock powder and ½ cup water. Reduce heat and simmer for 10 minutes, stirring occasionally. Add parsley and salt and pepper to taste. Spoon the meat sauce over the macaroni mixture.

For the cheese sauce, heat the butter in a small saucepan. Stir in the flour and cook, stirring, for 1 minute. Remove from heat and gradually add milk. Return to the heat, then stir until sauce boils and thickens, stirring occasionally. Add the cheese, parsley and egg and mix well.

Top the macaroni and meat sauce in the dish with the cheese sauce. Bake at 180°C for 30 minutes. Stand for 10 minutes before cutting into portions.

CHICKEN CACCIATORE

125 g button mushrooms
1 tablespoon oil
12 chicken drumsticks (about 1.2 kg)
1 medium onion, chopped
1 clove garlic, crushed
400 g tin tomatoes, puréed
½ cup white wine
½ cup chicken stock
1 teaspoon dried oregano
1 teaspoon dried thyme
Salt and pepper, to taste

Preheat oven to 180°C. Cut mushrooms into quarters. Heat oil in a heavy-based frying pan. Cook drumsticks in small batches over medium–high heat until well browned; transfer to a large ovenproof casserole dish.

Place the onion and garlic in a pan and cook over medium heat until golden. Spread over chicken. Add remaining ingredients to the pan and season to taste. Bring to the boil, reduce heat and simmer for 10 minutes. Pour mixture over chicken. Bake chicken, covered, for 35 minutes or until very tender.

VEAL CHOPS WITH SAGE AND LEMON

4 veal loin chops
Plain flour, for dusting
1 egg, beaten
2 tablespoons milk
1 tablespoon finely chopped sage or
    2 teaspoons dried sage
¾ cup dried breadcrumbs
30 g butter
1 tablespoon olive oil
1 clove garlic, crushed
Lemon wedges, to serve

Trim excess fat from the veal chops, curl up tails of chops and secure in place with toothpicks.

Place the flour in a plastic bag. Place chops, one at at time, in the bag and coat thoroughly with flour; shake off any excess. Place egg and milk in a shallow bowl and stir to combine. Combine sage and breadcrumbs on a plate. Dip the floured chops in the egg mixture, then press lightly into the breadcrumb mixture, coating thoroughly.

Heat butter, oil and garlic in a large frying pan. Add chops in a single layer; fry on both sides over medium heat until cooked through. Serve with lemon wedges.

MEXICAN-STYLE BEEF SPARE RIBS

1.5 kg beef spare ribs
2 bay leaves
¼ cup soft brown sugar
1 clove garlic, crushed

SAUCE
1 tablespoon vegetable oil
½ cup chopped onion
1 clove garlic, crushed
1 tablespoon sugar
2 tablespoons cider vinegar
425 g tin tomato purée
1 tablespoon Mexican-style chilli powder, or to taste
1 teaspoon dried oregano
1 teaspoon ground cumin
Hot pepper sauce, to taste

Place ribs and bay leaves in a large pan. Combine brown sugar and garlic with 1½ cups water and pour over ribs. Heat until boiling, then reduce heat, cover and simmer gently, turning ribs occasionally, until tender, 30–45 minutes.

For the sauce, heat the oil in a small pan, add onion and garlic and cook until soft. Stir in sugar, vinegar, purée, chilli powder, oregano, cumin and pepper sauce. Heat until boiling, reduce heat and simmer, stirring occasionally, for 5 minutes. Cover and keep warm.

Drain ribs and pat dry on paper towel. Grill about 13 cm above glowing coals, turning ribs and basting frequently with sauce, for 10–15 minutes. Serve with remaining sauce.

FISH AND CUMIN KEBABS

750 g skinless firm white fish fillets
2 tablespoons olive oil
1 garlic clove, crushed
3 tablespoons chopped coriander leaves
2 teaspoons ground cumin
1 teaspoon pepper

Cut the fish fillets into 3 cm cubes. Thread on oiled skewers and set them aside.

To make the marinade, combine the oil, garlic, coriander, cumin and pepper in a small bowl. Brush the marinade over the fish, cover with plastic wrap and refrigerate for several hours, or overnight, turning occasionally. Drain, reserving the marinade. Season just before cooking.

Put the skewers on a hot, lightly oiled barbecue flatplate. Cook for 5–6 minutes, or until tender, turning once and brushing with reserved marinade several times during cooking.

Suitable fish for this dish are blue-eye, snapper or perch.

SLOW-COOKED SHANKS

1 tablespoon oil
4 lamb shanks
2 red onions, sliced
10 cloves garlic, peeled
400 g tin chopped tomatoes
½ cup dry white wine
1 bay leaf
1 teaspoon grated lemon zest
1 large red capsicum, chopped
Salt and pepper
3 tablespoons chopped parsley

Preheat the oven to 170°C. Heat the oil in a large flameproof casserole dish, add the shanks in batches and cook over high heat until browned on all sides. Return all the lamb to the casserole.

Add the onion and garlic to the casserole and cook until softened. Add the tomato, wine, bay leaf, lemon zest, capsicum and ½ cup water and bring to the boil.

Cover the casserole and cook in the oven for 2–2½ hours, or until the meat is tender and falling off the bone and the sauce has thickened. Season to taste. Sprinkle the parsley over the top before serving. Serve with couscous or soft polenta.

PRAWN CURRY

1 tablespoon butter
1 onion, finely chopped
1 clove garlic, crushed
1½ tablespoons curry powder
2 tablespoons plain flour
2 cups skim milk
1 kg raw prawns, peeled and deveined
1½ tablespoons lemon juice
2 teaspoons sherry
1 tablespoon finely chopped parsley
Rice, to serve

Heat the butter in a large saucepan. Add the onion and garlic and cook for 5 minutes, or until softened. Add the curry powder and cook for 1 minute, then stir in the flour and cook for a further 1 minute.

Remove from heat and stir in the milk until smooth. Return to a low heat and stir constantly until the sauce has thickened. Simmer for 2 minutes and then stir in the prawns. Continue to simmer for 5 minutes, or until the prawns are just cooked.

Stir in the lemon juice, sherry and parsley and serve immediately with rice.

CHAPTER THREE

EVERYTHING I KNOW

ABOUT MAKING

SALADS AND VEGETABLE SIDES

BOXING DAY SALAD

DRESSING
½ cup mayonnaise
1 tablespoon lemon juice

500 g cooked turkey, diced
4 stalks celery, chopped
4 shallots, chopped
½ cup chopped nuts
½ red capsicum

To make dressing, blend mayonnaise and lemon juice. Combine all other ingredients then stir dressing through. Other seasonings may be added to the dressing, if desired.

POTATO BACON SALAD

2 kg washed new potatoes, unpeeled
250 g rindless bacon
Small bunch chives, chopped

DRESSING
300 ml sour cream
2 tablespoons vinegar
2 tablespoons milk, optional

If potatoes are small, cook whole, and if large, cut into bite-sized pieces. Do not overcook. Rinse under cold water. Drain and cool. Chop bacon and fry until golden, drain and cool.

To make dressing, mix ingredients until smooth. Combine with bacon and chives and pour over potatoes, mixing gently.

CURRIED VEGETABLE PASTA SALAD

500 g pasta shells or spirals
1 large carrot
1 small zucchini
¼ red capsicum
300 g broccoli, chopped
1 shallot, chopped
200 g button mushrooms, thickly sliced

DRESSING
1 small onion, chopped
Crushed garlic, to taste
1 teaspoon curry powder
Pinch turmeric
⅓ cup mustard pickles
½ cup low-fat mayonnaise
½ cup low-fat sour cream

To make the salad, boil the pasta and keep warm. Cut the carrot, zucchini and capsicum into long strips. Add the carrot and broccoli to boiling water and half-cook. Drain and combine all vegetables, including shallot and mushrooms, with the pasta.

To make the dressing, heat a pan and add the onion, garlic, curry, turmeric, pickles and 5 tablespoons water. Cook until onion softens. Combine mayonnaise and sour cream in a bowl, then add mixture to pan. Stir until the sauce thickens. Pour over pasta and vegetables and serve.

SALADS AND VEGETABLE SIDES

SEAFOOD SALAD AND SAUCE

500 g cooked prawns, peeled and deveined
150 g mixed lettuce leaves
2 large avocados, thinly sliced

DRESSING
¼ cup mayonnaise
¼ cup tomato sauce
¼ cup lightly whipped cream
¼ teaspoon curry powder
1 teaspoon lemon juice
1 teaspoon Worcestershire sauce
Salt and pepper, to taste

Combine prawns, lettuce and avocado. Combine all dressing ingredients and mix well. Drizzle salad with prepared dressing.

ZUCCHINI SALAD

500 g zucchini, diced
½ small red onion, finely chopped
1 medium tomato, finely diced
2-3 tablespoons basil leaves
1 tablespoon red wine vinegar
1 tablespoon oil
1 tablespoon lemon juice
Salt and pepper, to taste

Simmer zucchini for 2–3 minutes. Drain and cool. Combine with all other ingredients and toss gently.

SPINACH SALAD WITH DREAMY CREAMY DRESSING

2 large bunches English spinach
4 bacon rashers, trimmed
4 eggs, boiled
12 button mushrooms

DRESSING
½ cup mayonnaise
1 teaspoon sugar
1 teaspoon mustard
1 clove garlic
3 tablespoons lemon juice
½ cup sour cream
2 spring onions, including tops
1 tablespoon dried parsley
Salt and pepper, to taste

To make the salad, wash the spinach and chop finely. Cook the bacon until crisp; drain, allow to cool and chop finely. Coarsely chop the eggs. Clean and slice the mushrooms. Place all ingredients into a large salad bowl and refrigerate until ready to serve. Pour dressing over the salad and toss.

To make the dressing, place all ingredients in a blender and blend until the mixture is smooth. Refrigerate until ready to use. Dressing makes 1½ cups.

SALADS AND VEGETABLE SIDES

BACON AND AVOCADO SALAD

8 rindless bacon rashers
400 g green beans, trimmed and halved
300 g baby English spinach leaves
2 French shallots, finely sliced
2 avocados

DRESSING
¼ teaspoon brown sugar
1 clove garlic, crushed
⅓ cup olive oil
1 tablespoon balsamic vinegar
1 teaspoon sesame oil
Salt and pepper

Preheat the grill. Put the bacon on a tray and grill on both sides until it is nice and crisp. Leave to cool and then break into pieces.

Bring a saucepan of water to the boil and cook the beans for 4 minutes. Drain, then hold them under cold running water for a few seconds to stop them cooking any further.

Put the spinach in a large bowl and add the beans, bacon and shallots. Halve the avocados, then cut into cubes and add them to the bowl.

To make the dressing, mix the brown sugar and garlic in a small bowl. Add the rest of the ingredients and whisk everything together.

Pour the dressing over the salad and toss well. Grind some black pepper over the top and sprinkle with some salt.

CANNELLINI BEAN SALAD

425 g tin cannellini beans
1 tomato, finely chopped
3 anchovy fillets, sliced
1 tablespoon finely chopped red onion
2 teaspoons finely chopped basil
2 teaspoons extra virgin olive oil
1 teaspoon balsamic vinegar
Crusty bread, cut into slices, to serve
Olive oil, for brushing
1 garlic clove, bruised

Rinse and drain the cannellini beans. Combine the cannellini beans, tomato, anchovies, onion, basil, olive oil and balsamic vinegar.

Lightly brush the slices of bread with the oil, then toast and rub with the garlic. Spoon the salad onto the bread slices to serve.

HONEY-GLAZED CARROTS (MICROWAVE)

500 g carrots, finely diced
2 tablespoons honey
2 tablespoons orange juice
Pinch salt
1 tablespoon butter
2 tablespoons vinegar
2 teaspoons cornflour

Place carrots in a microwave-safe bowl with 1 tablespoon water. Microwave on high, covered, for 7 minutes, or less if more crisp carrots are preferred. Drain. Combine all other ingredients and microwave on high for 1 minute. Stir. Pour glaze over carrots and microwave on high for 2 minutes.

ROAST TOMATO SALAD

6 roma tomatoes
2 teaspoons capers
6 basil leaves, torn
1 tablespoon olive oil
1 tablespoon balsamic vinegar
2 garlic cloves, crushed
½ teaspoon honey
Salt and pepper

Cut the tomatoes into quarters lengthways. Cook, skin side down, on a hot barbecue grill plate or flat plate or under a kitchen grill for 4–5 minutes, or until golden. Cool to room temperature.

Combine the capers, basil, oil, vinegar, garlic and honey in a bowl, season with salt and pepper to taste, and pour over the tomatoes. Toss gently and serve immediately.

BAKED PUMPKIN CASSEROLE

1 kg pumpkin
1 heaped tablespoon plain flour
2 eggs, beaten
4 tablespoons milk
Salt and freshly ground black pepper
60 g grated cheese

Chop pumpkin into pieces, boil until tender, then mash. Sift flour, add eggs, milk and seasoning. Add pumpkin and cheese. Bake in a casserole dish, uncovered, in a moderate oven for 20–25 minutes.

BRAISED CABBAGE

1 onion
¼ cup bacon
1 teaspoon butter
3–4 cups shredded cabbage
Salt and pepper, to taste
1 tablespoon boiling water

Chop onion and bacon and lightly fry in butter. Add cabbage, salt and pepper. Add boiling water and cook gently for 10 minutes, stirring occasionally.

VARIATION: Add 2 teaspoons curry powder to 1 tablespoon boiling water and 1 tablespoon melted butter. Stir in chopped cabbage and cook for 5–10 minutes, stirring occasionally.

POTATO CASSEROLE (MICROWAVE)

3 large potatoes, sliced
3 bacon rashers, chopped
1 large onion, sliced
1½ cups grated tasty cheese
¾ cup cream
Paprika
30 g butter

In a well-greased microwave-safe casserole dish, place potato, bacon, onion and cheese in layers, repeating layers until all ingredients are used. Boil cream, then pour over potatoes. Sprinkle paprika on top and add a couple of small knobs of butter. Microwave on medium–high for 20 minutes.

POTATOES ROMANOFF

6 large potatoes (about 1.5 kg), peeled
600 g sour cream
8 shallots, chopped
125 g grated cheese, plus extra for sprinkling
Salt and pepper
Paprika

Cook potatoes until just tender, drain and cool. Coarsely grate potatoes into a large bowl. Add sour cream, shallots, grated cheese and salt and pepper. Place in a greased casserole dish; top with extra grated cheese and sprinkle with paprika. Cover and refrigerate overnight. Bake, uncovered, in a moderate oven for 45–50 minutes.

GRATED POTATO CAKES

3 large potatoes
1 small onion, grated
½ cup grated cheese
1 egg, lightly beaten
1 tablespoon plain flour
1 tablespoon wholegrain mustard
1 tablespoon chopped parsley
1 teaspoon powdered chicken stock
Salt and pepper, to taste
2 tablespoons oil, for shallow-frying

Peel and grate potatoes coarsely, squeeze out any excess moisture and dry between sheets of paper towel. Place all ingredients, except for the oil, in a bowl and mix thoroughly. Heat oil in a non-stick frying pan over medium heat and drop ¼ cups of mixture into oil (3 or 4 at a time). Flatten slightly and cook until brown on both sides. Not suitable to microwave or freeze.

ZUCCHINI BAKE

600 g zucchini, trimmed and grated (to give 4 cups)
4 eggs, beaten
¼ cup plain flour, sifted
½ cup grated cheese, plus extra for sprinkling
1 teaspoon salt
3 tablespoons chopped parsley
3 tablespoons sliced spring onion
1 clove garlic, crushed
¼ teaspoon pepper
1 punnet cherry tomatoes

Using paper towel, squeeze out as much moisture as possible from the zucchini. In a bowl, combine eggs, flour, cheese, salt, parsley, onion, garlic and pepper. Stir in zucchini and place mixture in a greased shallow baking dish. Cut tomatoes in half and place in dish with the cut side facing up. Sprinkle extra cheese over tomatoes, if desired. Bake, uncovered, at 180°C for 30 minutes or until mixture is set.

ZUCCHINI WITH GARLIC BUTTER

500 g zucchini
60 g butter
1 clove garlic, crushed
½ teaspoon salt
Pepper, to taste

Wash zucchini, remove ends, but do not peel. Shred coarsely. Melt butter, add garlic and stir for a few seconds. Add the zucchini and seasoning and toss in the butter for 4 minutes. Serve immediately.

SPINACH AND ORANGE SALAD

10 to 12 medium English spinach leaves
4 oranges, peeled
1 medium red onion, peeled and sliced thinly
½ cup pitted black olives, drained
¼ cup toasted pine nuts
⅓ cup olive oil
¼ cup red wine vinegar

Wash and dry spinach leaves. Remove large stems. Tear into bite-sized pieces. Segment oranges by carefully removing all white pith, leaving each segment bare of any skin at all. Add onion, olives and pine nuts. Whisk together olive oil and vinegar till well combined. Pour dressing over the salad and toss well. Best served as soon as possible.

CURRIED POTATO

6 large potatoes
1 large onion, chopped
1 tablespoon extra virgin olive oil
1 teaspoon curry powder, to taste
300 ml thickened cream

Peel potatoes and cut into 1 cm slices. Sauté onion in olive oil over medium heat until translucent. Remove from oil. Return oil to the heat and add curry powder. Quickly cook curry powder without burning it. Add cream and onion and remove from heat. Place potato slices in the bottom of a baking dish and pour over the cream mixture, making sure the mixture covers all pieces. Cook at 180°C for 25 minutes or until potato is tender. Increase the heat for the last 5 minutes, to brown the top.

MOROCCAN EGGPLANT

3–4 eggplants
1 kg roma tomatoes
3–4 teaspoons ground cumin
3–4 teaspoons ground coriander
3–4 teaspoons paprika
6–8 cloves garlic
1 bunch flat-leaf (Italian) parsley
Olive oil
½ cup red wine vinegar
Salt and freshly ground black pepper
¼ cup sundried tomatoes, chopped

Slice eggplants, spray slices with oil, then roast or grill. Season roma tomatoes and roast for 15 minutes at 200°C. Put spices on a tray lined with baking paper and toast in the oven for 5–8 minutes. Roughly chop garlic and parsley. Whisk oil and vinegar together and season. Combine eggplant slices, roma tomatoes, sundried tomatoes, spices and parsley (or you could use a mint and garlic mixture). Dress with vinaigrette and adjust seasoning.

SALADS AND VEGETABLE SIDES

ORIENTAL GINGER AND CASHEW RICE (MICROWAVE)

1 cup long-grain rice
2 cups hot water
30 g butter
1 clove garlic
½ cup raw cashews, chopped
¼ cup chopped glacé ginger
1 teaspoon grated lemon rind
¼ teaspoon ground cumin
2 tablespoons chopped mint

Combine rice and water in a large, shallow microwave-safe dish. Cook on high for 15 minutes, stirring occasionally. Combine butter, garlic and nuts in a dish and cook on high for 2 minutes. Stir. Combine rice, nut mixture and remaining ingredients; cook on high for about 3 minutes or until heated through, stir occasionally. Serves 4–6.

TOMATO AND CAPSICUM STEW

2 tablespoons olive oil
1 large red onion, chopped
2 large red capsicums, chopped
1 large green capsicum, chopped
4 large ripe tomatoes, peeled and chopped
2 teaspoons soft brown sugar

Heat oil in medium pan, add onion and cook over low heat until it is soft.

Add capsicums and cook over medium heat for 5 minutes, stirring constantly. Stir in tomato and brown sugar. Reduce heat, cover and cook for 6–8 minutes or until vegetables are tender.

TOMATO PUMPKIN

¼ pumpkin
1 medium onion
3 tablespoons tomato paste
2 cloves garlic, chopped
Salt and pepper, to taste
1 tablespoon olive oil, or to taste

Peel pumpkin and cut into 2 cm squares. Finely dice onion. Place cut pumpkin and onion into a baking dish and mix together with tomato paste, garlic, salt and pepper. Add olive oil and combine well. Bake in a moderate oven for about 30 minutes, stirring occasionally, until the pumpkin is just tender.

VEGETABLE SLICE

400 g mixed vegetables, roughly chopped (see Variation)
1 medium onion
1 cup grated tasty cheese
2 slices ham (optional)
1 cup self-raising flour, sifted
Salt and pepper, to taste
½ cup oil
4 eggs

Mix vegetables, onion, cheese, ham (if using), sifted flour and salt and pepper together. Add oil and eggs, lightly beaten. Line a slice pan with baking paper. Spoon mixture into pan and cook in a moderate oven for 30–40 minutes.

VARIATION: May use a packet of mixed chopped Chinese vegetables. Alternatively, this dish can be made with just a single vegetable.

ASPARAGUS STIR-FRIED WITH MUSTARD

480 g asparagus (see Variation)
1 tablespoon oil
1 red onion, sliced
1 garlic clove, crushed
1 tablespoon wholegrain mustard
1 teaspoon honey
125 ml cream

Break the woody ends off the asparagus. Cut the asparagus into 5 cm lengths.

Heat the wok until very hot, add the oil and swirl to coat the sides. Stir-fry the onion for 2–3 minutes, or until tender. Stir in the crushed garlic and cook for 1 minute. Add the asparagus to the wok and stir-fry for 3–4 minutes, or until tender, being careful not to overcook.

Remove the asparagus from the wok, set it aside and keep it warm. Combine the wholegrain mustard, honey and cream. Add to the wok and bring to the boil, then reduce the heat and simmer for 2–3 minutes, or until the mixture reduces and thickens slightly. Return the asparagus to the wok and toss it through the cream mixture. Serve immediately.

VARIATION: When asparagus is in season, white and purple asparagus are also available. Vary by using a mixture of the three colours. Do not overcook the purple asparagus or it will turn green.

Serve on croutons, toasted ciabatta or toasted wholegrain bread as an appetiser or first course.

VEGETABLES WITH HONEY AND SOY

1 tablespoon sesame seeds
1 tablespoon oil
1 teaspoon sesame oil
1 garlic clove, crushed
2 teaspoons grated fresh ginger
2 spring onions, thinly sliced
250 g broccoli, cut into small florets
1 red capsicum, thinly sliced
1 green capsicum, thinly sliced
150 g button mushrooms, halved
30 g pitted black olives, halved
1 tablespoon soy sauce
1 tablespoon honey
1 tablespoon sweet chilli sauce

Place the sesame seeds on an oven tray and toast under a hot grill for a couple of minutes, or until golden. Heat a wok, add the oils and swirl to coat the base and side of the wok. Add the garlic, ginger and spring onion and stir-fry for 1 minute.

Add the broccoli, capsicums, mushrooms and olives to the wok. Stir-fry for a further 2 minutes, or until the vegetables are just tender.

Combine the soy sauce, honey and chilli sauce in a bowl. Pour over the vegetables and then toss lightly. Sprinkle with the toasted sesame seeds and serve immediately.

TRICOLOUR PASTA SALAD

2 tablespoons olive oil, plus 1 tablespoon extra
2 tablespoons white wine vinegar
1 small clove garlic, halved
375 g tricolour pasta spirals
¾ cup sundried tomatoes in oil, drained
½ cup pitted black olives
100 g parmesan cheese
1 cup quartered artichoke hearts
½ cup shredded fresh basil leaves

Combine olive oil, vinegar and garlic in a small screw-top jar. Shake well then allow to stand for 1 hour.

Bring a large saucepan of water to the boil. Slowly add the pasta spirals and cook until just tender. Drain then toss with the extra olive oil while still hot. Allow to cool completely.

Cut sundried tomatoes into fine strips and cut olives in half. Shave parmesan cheese into paper-thin slices.

Place pasta, tomato, olives, cheese, artichokes and basil in a large serving bowl. Remove garlic halves from dressing and discard. Pour the dressing over the salad. Toss gently to combine.

CHAPTER FOUR

EVERYTHING I KNOW

ABOUT MAKING

DESSERTS

APPLE PIE

FILLING
6 green apples (about 1 kg), peeled and chopped
½ cup sugar
Juice of ½ lemon

PASTRY
125 g butter
½ cup caster sugar
1 egg
200 g plain flour
100 g self-raising flour

Stew apples with sugar, lemon juice and enough water to prevent sticking. Cool. For the pastry, beat butter and caster sugar; add egg and combine well. Add flours. Using fingers, press two-thirds of the mixture into a greased 20 x 30 cm lamington tin. Pour apple into uncooked pastry case; coarsely grate rest of rolled-out pastry over apple. Bake in moderate oven for 30 minutes or until golden.

BAKED APPLE PUDDING

60 g butter
¾ cup caster sugar
1 egg
Good pinch ground cloves
1 cup self-raising flour, sifted
¼ teaspoon bicarbonate of soda
3 cups thinly sliced apples

Cream butter and sugar. Combine with egg and cloves, then flour and bicarbonate of soda. Add apples and mix. Spoon into a greased baking dish. Bake in moderate oven for 50–60 minutes.

BREAD AND BUTTER PUDDING

30 g butter, softened
6 thin slices day-old white or brown bread,
    crusts removed
¾ cup mixed dried fruit
3 tablespoons caster sugar
1 teaspoon mixed spice
2 eggs, lightly beaten
1 teaspoon vanilla essence
2½ cups milk

Preheat oven to 180°C. Grease a medium-sized shallow ovenproof dish. Butter bread on one side and cut slices in half diagonally. Layer bread into the dish, sprinkling each layer with dried fruit, caster sugar and spice.

Beat the eggs, essence and milk together. Pour mixture over the bread and set aside for 5 minutes to soak. Bake pudding for 50 minutes, or until it is set and the top is browned.

MASCARPONE AND LIME TORTE

200 g packet ginger biscuits
50 g butter
2 limes
500 g mascarpone cheese
40 g icing sugar, sifted
50 g dark chocolate
Grapes, to garnish (optional)
50 g caster sugar (optional)

Grease an 18 cm springform cake tin and line the side with baking paper. Mix together crushed biscuits and melted butter. Press into the base of the tin. Finely zest the limes, then juice them. Place mascarpone, icing sugar, lime zest and juice in a bowl and beat together. Spread over biscuit base and chill for 30 minutes.

To decorate, grate chocolate over the top. If garnishing with grapes, dip grapes in water, shake off excess water, dip into caster sugar then arrange on torte. Serves 6–8.

MANGO FOOL

3 large mangoes
1 cup custard
1⅔ cups cream
Fresh fruit, to serve (optional)

Peel and stone mangoes and purée the flesh in a food processor. Add the custard and blend to combine.

Whip cream until soft peaks form, then gently fold into mango mixture until just combined. Do not overmix, as you want to end up with a marbled effect. Pour mixture into a serving dish or six glasses. Gently smooth the top, then refrigerate for at least 1 hour before serving. Serve with fresh fruit if desired.

PAVLOVA ROLL

Cornflour, for dusting
4 egg whites
¾ cup caster sugar, plus 1 tablespoon extra
1 teaspoon cinnamon
½ cup slivered almonds

FILLING
300 ml thickened cream, whipped
Grated chocolate, to taste

Grease and line a 26 x 32 cm Swiss roll tin, then dust with cornflour.
Beat egg whites until stiff, gradually adding caster sugar to form
a meringue. Spread meringue mixture into prepared tin. Sprinkle
combined sugar, cinnamon and almonds over meringue. Bake in a
moderate to moderately hot oven for 7–10 minutes, or until firm and
golden-tipped. Turn out onto baking paper resting on a cake cooler.
Cool for at least 5 minutes.

Beat cream until stiff, then fold in grated chocolate. Carefully
spread over meringue. Trim edges, then roll up from the long side
like a Swiss roll. Refrigerate until set. Decorate with confectionery,
if desired, and more grated chocolate.

VARIATION: Spread roll with strawberry jam, then lightly cover with
cream. Top with fresh halved strawberries and roll up. Decorate with
whole strawberries.

BUTTERMILK PANNACOTTA

20 g powdered gelatine
2½ cups cream
220 g caster sugar
400 ml buttermilk
2 teaspoons vanilla essence
Raspberry sauce, to serve

Sprinkle gelatine over ¼ cup water in a small heatproof bowl then place over a saucepan of simmering water and stir until gelatine has dissolved. Combine cream, sugar and buttermilk in another pan and heat gently until sugar has dissolved.

Remove from heat and stir in vanilla and gelatine until well combined. Pour into six 200 ml moulds rinsed out with cold water and chill, covered, for 4 hours or overnight, until set.

Turn pannacotta onto chilled plates. Serve with raspberry sauce or the sauce of your choice.

APRICOT LAYER PARFAIT

8 macaroons or small meringues
2 tablespoons sherry
400 g tin apricot halves, drained (see Variation)
⅔ cup whipped cream

Place 2 tablespoons of crushed macaroons in each of four dessert glasses. Sprinkle with a little sherry and spoon in a layer of chilled, drained apricot halves. Place 1 large tablespoon whipped cream on apricots. Repeat layers until all apricots are used and glass is filled.

VARIATION: Use 250 g strawberries instead of apricots.

BROWN SUGAR TART

SWEET COFFEE PASTRY
100 g caster sugar
180 g butter, chilled
300 g plain flour
½ cup cold coffee

FILLING
400 g brown sugar
1 teaspoon cornflour
4 eggs, beaten
100 ml cream
1 teaspoon vanilla essence
100 g melted butter

For the pastry, combine caster sugar, butter and flour in a food processor, and pulse into fine crumbs. Add coffee and bring together into a pliable dough. Wrap and chill for 30 minutes.

Roll pastry to fit a 30 cm loose-bottomed flan tin, trim and chill. Blind bake in a moderately hot oven for 10 minutes. Allow to cool before filling.

For the filling, combine sugar and cornflour, stir in eggs and mix well, followed by cream, vanilla and melted butter. Mix well.

Pour into tart case and bake in a low oven for about 1 hour or until custard is just set. Chill before serving with poached fruit.

ICE CREAM CAKE

375 g mixed fruit
½ cup brandy
1 madeira cake (about 450 g)
4 litres vanilla ice cream
125 g dark chocolate chips
Strawberries or 100 g packet glacé cherries, to decorate

Line two 10 x 22 x 8 cm deep loaf tins with foil or baking paper. Chop fruit and sprinkle with approximately 3 tablespoons brandy. Cut cake into cubes and sprinkle with remaining brandy. Soften ice cream and mix half of it with fruit, cake and chocolate chips. Spoon one quarter of the plain vanilla ice cream into each tin, pressing firmly and smoothing the top. Top each plain layer with half of the combined ice cream, cake and fruit mixture, pressing firmly and smoothing as before. Divide the remaining plain ice cream between the two tins and smooth the top.

Cover with foil or baking paper. Freeze until firm, preferably overnight. Remove from freezer 10–15 minutes before serving. Turn onto oblong platters. Decorate with cut strawberries or cherries. Each loaf serves about 10–12 when sliced. Any leftover mixture can be frozen separately for another occasion.

This recipe makes a generous quantity, so is handy for a party or large gathering.

BUTTERSCOTCH SELF-SAUCING PUDDING

Oil or butter, for brushing
90 g butter, softened
1 cup soft brown sugar
1½ cups self-raising flour, sifted
1 teaspoon mixed spice
¾ cup milk
60 g butter, extra
½ cup sugar

Preheat oven to 180°C. Brush six 1-cup capacity ovenproof dishes with oil or melted butter. Using electric beaters, beat butter and sugar in a small mixing bowl until light and creamy. Transfer to a large mixing bowl. Using a metal spoon, fold in sifted flour and mixed spice alternately with milk. Spoon evenly into dishes. Place on a baking tray.

Place extra butter, sugar and ¼ cup water in a small pan. Stir over low heat until butter has melted and sugar has dissolved. Bring to boil, reduce heat and simmer gently, uncovered, until golden brown. Remove from heat. Very carefully stir in 1 cup water. Stir over low heat until smooth; allow to cool slightly.

Pour an equal amount of the butterscotch mixture over each pudding. Bake for 35 minutes, or until a skewer inserted halfway into the centre of the pudding comes out clean. Loosen each pudding by running a knife around the edge. Invert onto serving plates.

BAKED RICE CUSTARD

Melted butter or oil, for brushing
¼ cup short-grain rice
2 eggs
¼ cup caster sugar
1½ cups milk
½ cup cream
1 teaspoon vanilla extract
1–2 teaspoons grated lemon zest
¼ cup sultanas or currants (optional)
¼ teaspoon ground cinnamon or nutmeg

Preheat the oven to 160°C. Brush a deep 20 cm round ovenproof dish with melted butter or oil. Cook rice in a medium pan of boiling water until just tender and drain.

In a medium bowl, whisk the eggs, sugar, milk, cream, vanilla and zest for about 2 minutes. Fold in the cooked rice and sultanas or currants, if using. Pour mixture into prepared dish. Sprinkle with nutmeg or cinnamon.

Place filled dish into a deep baking dish. Pour in water to come halfway up the side of the baking dish. Bake for 50 minutes or until custard is set and a knife comes out clean when inserted in the centre. Remove the dish from the baking dish immediately. Allow to stand for 5 minutes before serving. Serve the custard with cream or stewed fruits.

PASSIONFRUIT MOUSSE

5–6 passionfruit
6 eggs, separated
185 g caster sugar
½ teaspoon finely grated lemon zest
3 tablespoons lemon juice
1 tablespoon gelatine
315 ml cream, lightly whipped
40 g flaked coconut, toasted

Cut the passionfruit in half and scoop out the pulp. Strain, reserving the seeds and pulp, then measure out 3 tablespoons juice and set aside. Add the seeds and pulp to the remaining juice and set aside.

Put the egg yolks, 125 g of the sugar, the lemon zest, lemon juice and strained passionfruit juice in a heatproof bowl. Put the bowl over a saucepan of simmering water and, using electric beaters, beat for 10 minutes, or until thick and creamy. Remove from the heat and transfer to a glass bowl.

Sprinkle the gelatine over 125 ml water in a small bowl and leave until spongy. Put the bowl in a pan of just-boiled water (the water should come halfway up the side of the bowl) and stir until dissolved. Add the gelatine to the mousse mixture and combine well. Mix in the passionfruit pulp and leave until cold, then fold in the lightly whipped cream.

Using electric beaters, whisk the egg whites until soft peaks form. Gradually whisk in the remaining sugar, beating until it has dissolved. Fold the egg whites into the mousse mixture quickly and lightly. Spoon into eight 250 ml ramekins or stemmed wine glasses. Refrigerate for 2 hours, or until set. Sprinkle with the coconut just before serving.

MANGO AND PASSIONFRUIT PIES

750 g ready-made sweet shortcrust pastry
3 mangoes, peeled and sliced or chopped,
    or 400 g tinned mango slices, drained
60 g passionfruit pulp, strained
1 tablespoon custard powder
90 g caster sugar
1 egg, lightly beaten
Icing sugar, to dust
Cream, to serve

Preheat the oven to 190°C. Grease six 10 x 8 x 3 cm fluted flan tins or round pie dishes. Roll out two-thirds of the pastry between two sheets of baking paper to a thickness of 3 mm. Cut out six 13 cm circles, line the tins with them and trim the edges. Refrigerate while you make the filling.

Combine the mango, passionfruit, custard powder and caster sugar in a bowl.

Roll out the remaining pastry, including the trimmings, between two sheets of baking paper to 3 mm thick. Cut out six 11 cm circles. Re-roll the pastry trimmings and cut into shapes for decoration.

Fill the pastry cases with the mango mixture and brush the edges with egg. Top with the pastry circles and press the edges to seal. Trim the edges and decorate with the pastry shapes. Brush the tops with beaten egg and dust with icing sugar.

Bake for 20–25 minutes, or until golden brown. Serve with cream.

LEMON DELICIOUS

70 g unsalted butter, at room temperature
185 g sugar
2 teaspoons finely grated lemon zest
3 eggs, separated
30 g self-raising flour
185 ml milk
4 tablespoons lemon juice
Icing sugar, to dust
Thick cream, to serve

Preheat the oven to 180°C. Melt 10 g of the butter and use to lightly grease a 1.25 litre ovenproof ceramic dish.

Using electric beaters, beat the remaining butter, the sugar and grated zest together in a bowl until light and creamy. Gradually add the egg yolks, beating well after each addition. Fold in the flour and milk alternately to make a smooth but still runny batter. Stir in the lemon juice.

In another bowl, whisk the egg whites until firm peaks form and, with a large metal spoon, fold one-third of the whites into the batter. Gently fold in the remaining egg whites, being careful not to overmix.

Pour the batter into the prepared dish and place it in a large roasting tin. Pour enough hot water into the tin to come one-third of the way up the side of the roasting tin. Bake for 55 minutes, or until the top of the pudding is golden, risen and firm to the touch. Leave for 5 minutes before serving. Dust the pudding with icing sugar and serve with cream.

PEACH PIE

500 g ready-made sweet shortcrust pastry
1.65 kg tinned peach slices, well drained
125 g caster sugar
30 g cornflour
¼ teaspoon almond essence
20 g unsalted butter, chopped
1 tablespoon milk
1 egg, lightly beaten
Caster sugar, for sprinkling

Roll out two-thirds of the dough between two sheets of baking paper until large enough to line a 23 x 18 x 3 cm pie dish. Remove the top sheet of paper and invert the pastry into the dish. Use a small ball of pastry to press the pastry into the dish. Trim any excess pastry with a knife. Refrigerate for 20 minutes.

Preheat the oven to 200°C. Line the pastry with crumpled baking paper and pour in baking beads or rice. Bake for 10 minutes, remove the paper and beads and return to the oven for 5 minutes, or until the pastry base is dry and lightly coloured. Allow to cool.

Mix the peaches, sugar, cornflour and almond essence in a bowl, then spoon into the pastry shell. Dot with butter and moisten edges of the pastry with milk.

Roll out the remaining dough to a 25 cm square. Using a fluted pastry cutter, cut into ten strips 2.5 cm wide. Lay the strips in a lattice pattern over the filling, pressing firmly on the edges, and trim. Brush with egg and sprinkle with sugar. Bake for 10 minutes, reduce the heat to 180°C and bake for 30 minutes more, or until golden. Cool before serving.

GRANDMOTHER'S PAVLOVA

4 egg whites
Pinch salt
230 g caster sugar
2 teaspoons cornflour
1 teaspoon white vinegar
500 ml cream
3 passionfruit, to decorate
Strawberries, to decorate

Preheat the oven to 160°C. Line a 32 x 28 cm baking tray with baking paper.

Place the egg whites and salt in a dry bowl. Using electric beaters, beat until stiff peaks form. Add the sugar gradually, beating constantly after each addition, until mixture is thick and glossy and all sugar is dissolved.

Using a metal spoon, fold in the cornflour and vinegar. Spoon the mixture into a mound on the prepared tray. Lightly flatten the top of the pavlova and smooth the sides. (This pavlova should have a cake shape and be about 2.5 cm high.) Bake for 1 hour, or until pale cream in colour and crisp. Remove from the oven while warm and carefully turn upside down onto a plate. Allow to cool.

Lightly whip the cream until soft peaks form and spread over the soft centre of the pavlova. Decorate with passionfruit pulp and halved strawberries. Cut into wedges to serve.

SELF-SAUCING CHOCOLATE PUDDING

Melted butter, for brushing
1 cup self-raising flour
3 tablespoons cocoa powder
½ cup caster sugar
1 egg
½ cup milk
60 g butter, melted
1 teaspoon vanilla essence
1 cup soft brown sugar
1½ cups boiling water
Whipped cream or ice-cream, to serve

Preheat the oven to 180°C. Brush a 2-litre heatproof dish with melted butter. Sift the flour and 1 tablespoon cocoa into a large bowl and add the sugar. Make a well in the mixture.

Beat the egg in a jug and add the milk, melted butter and vanilla essence. Pour the liquid into the dry ingredients and, using a wooden spoon, stir the batter until it is well combined and lump free. Pour into the prepared dish.

Combine the brown sugar and the remaining cocoa and sprinkle evenly over the batter. Pour the boiling water gently and evenly over the ingredients in the dish. Bake for 30–40 minutes, or until the pudding is cooked—a sauce will have formed underneath. Serve hot with whipped cream or ice cream.

For a crunchy alternative, add half a cup of chopped walnuts to the pudding batter before baking.

RHUBARB AND PEAR CRUMBLE

600 g rhubarb
2 strips lemon zest
1 tablespoon honey, or to taste
2 firm, ripe pears
½ cup rolled oats
¼ cup wholemeal plain flour
⅓ cup soft brown sugar
50 g butter

Trim the rhubarb, wash and cut into 3 cm pieces. Place in a medium pan with the lemon zest and 1 tablespoon water. Cook, covered, over low heat for 10 minutes, or until tender. Cool a little. Stir in the honey and remove the lemon zest.

Preheat the oven to 180°C. Peel and core the pears and cut into 2 cm cubes. Combine with the rhubarb. Pour into a 1.25 litre dish and smooth the surface.

To make the topping, combine the oats, flour and brown sugar in a bowl. Rub in the butter with your fingertips until the mixture is crumbly. Spread over the fruit. Bake for 15 minutes, or until cooked and golden.

CHERRY STRUDEL

470 g tin or jar pitted cherries, drained
¾ cup very finely chopped walnuts
½ cup caster sugar
1 tablespoon grated lemon zest
1 teaspoon ground cinnamon
1 teaspoon ground allspice
¾ cup fresh white breadcrumbs
¼ cup melted butter, plus extra for brushing
1 sheet frozen puff pastry, thawed
Poppy seeds, for sprinkling (optional)
Whipped cream, for serving

Halve cherries and set aside in a colander to drain. Combine walnuts, sugar, zest, cinnamon and allspice in a large bowl.

In another bowl, combine breadcrumbs and melted butter. Add breadcrumb mixture to nut mixture; stir well.

Lay the sheet of pastry on a work surface and brush with a little melted butter. Spread with breadcrumb mixture, then cherries, leaving a 5 cm margin on each side. Fold over lengthways and press edges together firmly. Tuck in short ends. Brush all over with melted butter and sprinkle with poppy seeds if using. Place on a greased oven tray and bake for 10 minutes in a hot oven, then reduce heat to moderate and bake for a further 25–30 minutes or until golden. Serve warm with whipped cream.

CHAPTER FIVE

EVERYTHING I KNOW

ABOUT BAKING

CAKES

DATE LOAF

1 teaspoon bicarbonate of soda
1 cup boiling water
1 cup chopped dates
1 tablespoon butter, softened
¾ cup brown sugar
1 egg, lightly beaten
1½ cups plain flour, sifted
1 teaspoon cinnamon

Mix bicarbonate of soda in boiling water and add to dates in a bowl. Allow to cool. Cream butter and brown sugar, then add egg and prepared date mixture. Stir in flour and cinnamon. Place mixture in a greased and lined loaf tin and bake in a moderate oven for approximately 1 hour.

PUMPKIN LOAF

2 tablespoons butter, softened
¾ cup caster sugar
1 teaspoon vanilla essence
1 cup cold mashed pumpkin
2 cups self-raising flour, sifted
Pinch salt
¾ cup milk
2 tablespoons chopped walnuts
1 cup sultanas

Mix butter and sugar, then add vanilla and pumpkin. Fold in sifted flour, salt, milk, nuts and sultanas. Mix well. Bake in a well-greased and lightly floured 20 x 12 x 7 cm loaf tin or 2 smaller tins in a moderate oven on centre shelf for 30–45 minutes depending on size of tin. Serve cold, sliced and buttered.

IRENE'S DATE AND WALNUT LOAF

1 tablespoon butter, softened
1 cup brown sugar
1 egg
1 cup chopped dates
1 teaspoon bicarbonate of soda
1 cup boiling water
140 g chopped walnuts
2 cups plain flour, sifted
1 teaspoon baking powder

Mix together butter and brown sugar, then add egg. Over medium heat, beat together dates, bicarbonate of soda and water until thick. Add walnuts. Combine with butter mixture, along with sifted flour and baking powder. Bake in a greased and lined loaf tin in a moderate oven for approximately 1 hour. Slice loaf and spread with butter.

FRUIT LOAF

1 cup cold tea
1 cup sugar (brown or white)
1 cup mixed dried fruit
2 cups self-raising flour, sifted

Soak together tea, sugar and fruit for 2 hours. Fold in sifted flour. Bake in a greased and lined bar cake tin in a moderate oven for 40–50 minutes.

ANGEL FOOD CAKE

4 large egg whites
½ teaspoon cream of tartar
Vanilla
⅔ cup caster sugar
¼ cup plain flour
1 tablespoon cornflour
Pinch salt
Whipped cream, to serve
Strawberries, to serve

Dust a deep 20 cm ring tin with flour or line bottom with baking paper; do not grease. Beat egg whites until foamy, add cream of tartar, beat until very stiff, then add a little vanilla. Sift together sugar and flours. Carefully fold dry ingredients, 2 tablespoonfuls at a time, into egg whites. Spoon mixture into tin and bake in moderate oven for about 25 minutes. Remove from oven; leave in tin until cold. Cover with cream and strawberries.

QUICK LIGHT FRUIT CAKE

470 g plain flour
1 teaspoon baking powder
250 g butter, softened
250 g caster sugar
4 large eggs
1 teaspoon vanilla
Pinch salt
375 g mixed dried fruit

Sift flour and baking powder. Place all ingredients except mixed fruit in large bowl and beat until creamy. Fold in fruit. Spoon into greased and lined deep 20 cm round tin. Bake in low oven for 1¾ hours.

CHOCOLATE CAKE

125 g butter, softened
1 cup caster sugar
2 eggs
170 g self-raising flour
2 tablespoons cocoa
½ cup milk
¼ teaspoon vanilla
2 tablespoons boiling water

Cream butter and sugar. Add eggs; beat well after each addition. Sift flour and cocoa together. Fold half sifted flour and cocoa into creamed mixture, then milk and vanilla, then remaining sifted flour mixture. Stir in boiling water last. Bake in a greased and lined deep 17 cm round cake tin or a square tin in a moderate oven for 40–45 minutes.

BANANA CAKE

125 g butter, softened
¾ cup caster sugar
2 eggs
1½ cups plain flour
1 teaspoon baking powder
Pinch salt
3 ripe bananas, mashed and sprinkled with
    1 teaspoon lemon juice
6 dates, chopped (optional)

Cream together butter and sugar, then add eggs, one at a time, and beat well. Sift flour, baking powder and salt. Add a little of the flour mixture to the creamed mixture before adding bananas and lemon juice. Add remaining flour and dates, if using. Bake in a greased and lined deep 20 cm ring tin in a moderate oven for 35–40 minutes.

BANANA SPONGE

4 eggs, separated
¾ cup caster sugar
2 ripe bananas, well mashed
½ cup cornflour
¾ cup plain flour
1 teaspoon cream of tartar
Pinch salt
½ teaspoon bicarbonate of soda
4 tablespoons hot water
Whipped cream, to fill

Beat egg whites in a medium bowl until stiff, gradually add sugar and beat for 5 minutes. Add egg yolks and bananas and beat for 1 minute. Fold in well-sifted flours, cream of tartar and salt. Fold in bicarbonate of soda dissolved in hot water. Pour into two greased and lined 22 cm round sandwich tins and bake in a moderate oven for 25 minutes. Turn out onto wire racks to cool, then sandwich the cakes with whipped cream.

BANANA BLUEBERRY CAKE

125 g butter, softened
1 cup caster sugar
1 teaspoon vanilla
2 eggs
2 cups self-raising flour, sifted
⅓ cup sour cream or thick yoghurt
1 cup mashed bananas
½ cup blueberries

Place butter, sugar and vanilla in a bowl and beat until light and creamy. Add eggs and beat well. Fold through sifted flour, sour cream, bananas and finally blueberries; do not crush them. Spoon mixture into a 22 cm greased and lined round cake tin and bake in preheated moderate oven for about 1 hour. Cool in tin.

PUMPKIN MUFFINS

2 cups self-raising flour, sifted
¼ teaspoon cinnamon
¼ teaspoon nutmeg
½ teaspoon bicarbonate of soda
¼ cup brown sugar
¼ cup chopped raisins
1 egg
½ cup milk
¼ cup oil
1 cup mashed pumpkin

Mix all dry ingredients in a bowl. Add egg, milk, oil and pumpkin. Mix in lightly. Bake in greased muffin tins in a moderate oven for 25–30 minutes.

BEETROOT CAKE

250 g butter, softened
1 cup caster sugar
4 eggs
250 g fresh beetroot
150 g currants
2 teaspoons grated lemon zest
1 tablespoon lemon juice
1 cup plain flour
1 cup self-raising flour
½ teaspoon nutmeg

Grease a 14 x 21 cm loaf tin and line the base with paper. Cream butter and sugar until light and fluffy. Beat in eggs one at a time. Add peeled and finely chopped beetroot, currants, lemon zest and juice and half of the flours sifted with the nutmeg. Mix well. Stir in remaining sifted flours. Spread mixture in tin. Bake in a moderate oven for about 1½ hours. Allow to stand for 5 minutes before turning out.

TWO-AT-A-TIME CAKE

500 g self-raising flour
400 g caster sugar
5 eggs
1½ cups milk
1 teaspoon vanilla
250 g butter or margarine, softened

Sift flour and sugar together. Add eggs, milk, vanilla and butter. Beat together for 5 minutes. Pour into two greased and lined 20 cm round cake tins. Bake in a moderate oven for 30 minutes or until cooked when tested with a skewer.

CARROT AND SULTANA CAKE

2 eggs
¾ cup caster sugar
¾ cup oil
½ teaspoon vanilla
1 teaspoon bicarbonate of soda
½ teaspoon mixed spice
½ teaspoon salt
1 cup plain flour
1½ cups finely grated carrots, lightly packed
½ cup sultanas and/or ½ cup chopped walnuts

Combine eggs, sugar, oil and vanilla, then sift in dry ingredients. Beat at a low speed until smooth. Stir in carrots, sultanas and/or walnuts. Mix well and pour mixture into a greased and lined 20 x 10 x 7 cm loaf tin. Bake in a moderate oven for 40–45 minutes.

POTATO FRUIT BUN

60 g butter
½ cup caster sugar
½ cup cold mashed potato
1 egg
1 cup mixed dried fruit or sultanas
1 cup self-raising flour, sifted
¼ cup milk
½ teaspoon vanilla

Cream butter and sugar, then add mashed potato. Beat until well mixed. Add egg and fruit, then add sifted flour alternately with the milk and vanilla. Place in a greased and lined 20 x 10 x 7 cm loaf tin. Bake in moderate oven for 30–35 minutes.

CRUNCHY COFFEE CAKE

125 g butter
½ cup sugar
2 eggs
1¼ cups self-raising flour, sifted
3 tablespoons milk
½ teaspoon vanilla

TOPPING
4 tablespoons self-raising flour
2 tablespoons melted butter
2 teaspoons cinnamon
1 tablespoon desiccated coconut
2 tablespoons brown sugar

Cream butter and sugar until light, then add well-beaten eggs. Fold in sifted flour alternately with milk and vanilla. Spoon into a greased and lined deep 20 cm round tin.

For topping, sift flour and combine with other ingredients and sprinkle over mixture. Bake in a moderate oven for 45 minutes.

BASIC BUTTER CAKE

125 g butter, softened
1 cup caster sugar
1½ cups self-raising flour, sifted
½ teaspoon salt
2 eggs
A little more than 1 cup milk

In a bowl, beat all ingredients at medium speed for 4 minutes. Bake in a greased and lined 20 cm round cake tin at 180°C for 40–45 minutes.

VARIATIONS: **Orange cake** – Add grated zest of 1 orange. **Chocolate cake** – Replace 2 rounded tablespoons of flour with same quantity of cocoa. **Base for lamingtons** – Bake in a square cake tin or lamington tin.

QUICK MIX CAKE

¼ cup milk
80 g soft butter or margarine
¾ cup caster sugar
2 eggs
1 cup self-raising flour
1 tablespoon cornflour
½ teaspoon vanilla (or to taste)
Pinch salt

Preheat oven to 180°C. Place all ingredients in a bowl and beat well for 5 minutes at medium speed. Spoon into a greased and lined 20 x 10 cm loaf tin. Bake for 35 minutes or until a skewer comes out clean. Leave in the tin for a few minutes before turning out. When cold, ice as desired.

CHOCOLATE MACAROON CAKE

MACAROON
1 egg white
Pinch salt
½ cup caster sugar
2 cups desiccated coconut
1 tablespoon plain flour
¼ cup chopped walnuts

CAKE
125 g butter, softened
1 cup caster sugar
2 eggs
2 cups self-raising flour
2 tablespoons cocoa
1 cup milk
1 teaspoon vanilla

ICING
2 cups icing sugar
1 heaped tablespoon cocoa
35 g butter, softened
Milk, to mix
Walnuts, to decorate

To make the macaroon, beat egg white with salt until mixture holds its shape. Beat in sugar. Mix coconut with plain flour and mix into egg white mixture. If the mixture is crumbly, add 1 tablespoon water. Add walnuts and divide mixture into two equal portions.

To make cake, cream butter and sugar until light and fluffy. Add eggs one at a time and mix through. Sift flour and cocoa together and add about one-third of the creamed mixture. Add one-third of the combined milk and vanilla and continue adding, alternating ingredients until combined. Grease a deep 20 cm round tin. Spoon one-third of cake mixture into the tin, spreading evenly, then half the macaroon mixture, then another third of cake mixture, the rest of macaroon mixture and then the remaining cake mixture. Bake in a moderate oven for 1 hour or until cooked when tested with a skewer.

To make the icing, sift the icing sugar and cocoa, then mix in butter and milk until consistency is easy to spread. Decorate the iced cake with chopped walnuts.

CHOCOLATE RIPPLE CAKE

125 g butter, softened
¾ cup caster sugar
2 eggs
1½ cups self-raising flour
⅔ cup milk

RIPPLE MIXTURE
1 tablespoon cocoa
¼ cup caster sugar
⅓ cup chopped walnuts
½ tablespoon butter

Cream butter and sugar, add eggs and beat well. Sift flour and add alternately with milk. Spoon half the mixture into a greased and lined 20 cm ring tin. Combine ripple mixture ingredients and then crumble over the cake mixture into the tin. Place remaining cake mixture on top. Bake in a moderate oven for 35 minutes or until cooked. Ice with chocolate ganache or as desired.

DUTCH CAKE

3 tablespoons butter, softened
½ cup caster sugar
1 egg
¼ cup self-raising flour
1 teaspoon mixed spice
1 teaspoon cinnamon
¼ teaspoon nutmeg
¼ cup desiccated coconut
¼ cup mixed fruit
¼ cup chopped nuts
½ cup milk

Cream butter and sugar, then beat in egg. Sift together all dry ingredients and fold in with coconut, fruit, nuts and milk. Pour into a greased and lined 18 cm cake tin and bake in moderate oven for 30–40 minutes. Ice with lemon icing (see below).

LEMON ICING

2 tablespoons milk, at room temperature, plus extra
    as needed
2 teaspoons lemon juice
2 teaspoons butter, softened
200 g icing sugar
1 teaspoon grated lemon rind

Combine milk, lemon juice, butter and sifted icing sugar and beat well. Add lemon zest last. Add more icing sugar or more milk, to thicken or thin if needed.

FRUIT CAKE

1 kg mixed dried fruit
100 g glacé cherries
75 g walnuts
⅓ cup rum
250 g butter, softened
250 g brown sugar
5 eggs
1 teaspoon vanilla essence
1 tablespoon golden syrup
340 g plain flour
1 small teaspoon baking powder
1 teaspoon cinnamon
1 teaspoon mixed spice

Combine dried fruit, cherries, walnuts and rum, cover and leave overnight. Prepare a 22 cm round or square cake tin. Grease tin and line with several layers of newspaper and two layers of baking paper. Cream butter and sugar. Add eggs one at a time, beating well after each addition. Add essence and golden syrup. Sift dry ingredients. Add dry ingredients alternately with fruit to creamed mixture. Spoon mixture into the prepared tin. Bake in a low oven for 1 hour, then reduce to a very low oven for 2 hours.

GINGER SPONGE

¾ cup caster sugar
5 eggs
1 tablespoon golden syrup
⅓ cup self-raising flour
⅓ cup cornflour
3 teaspoons ground ginger
1 teaspoon ground cinnamon
2 teaspoons cocoa

ICING

125 g butter, softened
250 g icing sugar
2 teaspoons boiling water

Beat the sugar and eggs for 8 minutes or until mixture holds its shape. Add golden syrup and beat through to combine. Sift dry ingredients together three times. Add dry mixture to the liquid mixture and stir to combine. Bake in two greased and lined 22 cm sandwich tins in a moderate oven for 20 minutes. Do not open the oven door during that time.

To make buttercream icing, beat butter until smooth. Gradually add the icing sugar, mixing well, then add the water and mix well.

HONEY ROLL

4 eggs
110 g brown sugar
60 g caster sugar, plus extra for sprinkling
2 teaspoons honey
140 g self-raising flour
½ teaspoon cinnamon
¼ teaspoon bicarbonate of soda
15 g cornflour
1 teaspoon butter
2 tablespoons hot water
Mock cream (see below) or whipped cream

Beat eggs in a medium bowl until thick, add sugars slowly and beat until light and thick. While beating, add honey. Sift dry ingredients several times and fold in lightly. Melt butter in hot water and fold in. Prepare a Swiss roll tin and line with baking paper. Pour mixture into the tin and bake in a moderate oven for about 25 minutes. Do not overcook, as this mixture burns easily. Turn out onto paper or cloth sprinkled with caster sugar. Trim edges and carefully roll up tightly. When cooled, unroll and fill with mock or whipped cream, then reroll.

MOCK CREAM

2 cups sugar
120 g butter
½ teaspoon vanilla

Heat sugar and ⅓ cup water in a saucepan, stirring constantly over heat until sugar is dissolved. Increase heat and bring to the boil. Remove from heat and allow to cool completely. Beat butter and vanilla until white and fluffy, then gradually pour in cold syrup, beating constantly. Refrigerate until ready for use.

KENTISH CAKE

170 g butter, softened
¾ cup caster sugar
2 eggs
1 cup self-raising flour
2 tablespoons desiccated coconut
2 tablespoons cocoa
¼ cup milk
90 g sultanas, nuts and cherries

Cream butter and sugar, then add eggs, beating well after each addition. Fold in sifted dry ingredients, add the milk, fruit and nuts. Bake in a deep greased and lined 20 cm round cake tin or a 14 x 21 cm loaf tin for 45 minutes, or until cooked. Turn out onto a wire rack to cool then ice with caramel or chocolate icing.

NORWEGIAN SOUR CREAM CAKE

2 eggs
2 cups caster sugar
2 cups sour cream
3 cups plain flour
1 teaspoon bicarbonate of soda
½ teaspoon cinnamon
½ teaspoon cardamom
2 or 3 drops almond essence

Beat eggs and sugar until creamy, then add sour cream and well-sifted dry ingredients in alternate lots. Add almond essence. Blend well. Grease a 24 cm ring tin and line with baking paper. Pour mixture into tin and bake in a moderate oven for 55–60 minutes. When cooked, leave in tin for 10 minutes before turning out. Serve plain or spread with butter.

LEMON TEA CAKE

1½ cups plain flour
¼ teaspoon salt
1 teaspoon baking powder
1 cup caster sugar
125 g butter, chilled and cubed
2 eggs, beaten
½ cup milk
Grated zest and juice of 1 lemon
½ cup chopped walnuts
¼ cup sugar, extra

Grease a 20 cm ring tin and line base with baking paper. Sift flour, salt and baking powder into a bowl. Add sugar. Rub in the butter until it resembles fine breadcrumbs, or use a food processor to achieve this result. Combine eggs and milk, stir into mixture, then fold in lemon zest and walnuts. Spoon mixture into the tin and bake in a moderate oven for about 1 hour. Mix the lemon juice and extra sugar in a cup and pour over cake as soon as it is removed from the oven. Allow to cool in tin.

MACAROON CAKE

115 g butter, softened
115 g caster sugar
3 egg yolks
½ cup milk
1 teaspoon vanilla
180 g self-raising flour, sifted

TOPPING
3 egg whites
115 g caster sugar
115 g desiccated coconut

Cream butter and sugar, then add egg yolks and beat. Add milk, vanilla and sifted flour and stir well. Place in a well-greased and lined 20 x 30 cm lamington tin or rectangular slice tin.

To make topping, beat egg whites until stiff. Add sugar and beat well. Add coconut. Mix well and spread over cake mixture. Bake in a moderate oven for approximately 45 minutes.

MARBLE CAKE

120 g butter, softened
250 g caster sugar
3 eggs
1 cup self-raising flour
1 cup plain flour
¾ cup milk, at room temperature
1 teaspoon vanilla essence
1 rounded tablespoon cocoa
2 tablespoons hot water
Pink food colouring

Cream butter and sugar well, then add eggs one at a time, beating well after each addition. Fold in sifted flours alternately with the milk and vanilla. Divide mixture into three equal parts. Colour one part chocolate with the cocoa mixed with hot water and allowed to cool. Add pink colouring to second portion and leave third portion plain. Place alternate spoonfuls of mixture into a greased and lined deep 20 cm round or square tin. Shake down and run a knife through mixture to give a marbled effect. Bake in a moderate oven for about 1 hour or until a skewer inserted in the centre comes out clean. When cooked leave in tin for a few minutes before removing. Ice as desired.

This colourful cake is popular for children's birthday parties.

MOIST COCONUT CAKE

125 g butter, softened
1 cup caster sugar
½ teaspoon coconut essence
2 eggs
½ cup desiccated coconut
1½ cups self-raising flour, sifted
300 g sour cream
⅓ cup milk

COCONUT-ICE FROSTING
2 cups icing sugar
2 egg whites, lightly beaten
1⅓ cups desiccated coconut
Pink food colouring

Grease a 23 cm round cake tin, then line base with paper. Cream butter and sugar, add coconut essence, then beat in eggs one at a time, combining well. Stir in half the coconut and sifted flour with half the sour cream and milk, then stir in all remaining ingredients. Bake in a moderate oven for about 1 hour. When cool, ice the cake with coconut-ice frosting.

To make frosting, combine sifted icing sugar with egg whites, mix well, add coconut and a little colouring.

CHAPTER SIX

EVERYTHING I KNOW

ABOUT BAKING

SCONES, BISCUITS AND SLICES

PLAIN SCONES

¾ cup cream
1 cup milk
3 rounded tablespoons icing sugar, sifted
3 cups self-raising flour, sifted

With a rotary beater, beat together cream, milk and icing sugar for
1 minute. Add sifted flour and combine. Press onto a flat surface and
cut into desired shapes. Place on a greased and floured baking tray
and cook in a hot oven for 12–15 minutes.

POTATO SCONES

1½ cups self-raising flour
1 cup cold mashed potato
30 g butter
¾–1 cup milk, plus extra
½ cup coarsely grated tasty cheese

Sift flour into a bowl, add mashed potato and stir to combine. Add
butter and milk and mix to form a soft dough. Turn onto a lightly
floured surface. Knead dough lightly. Divide into eight portions. Roll
each into a thin sausage, about 25 cm long. Shape the rolls into knots
and place on a baking tray that has been dusted with flour.

Brush tops of knots with extra milk and sprinkle with grated
cheese. Bake in a hot oven for 15–20 minutes or until scones are
golden and cooked through. Serve scones warm, spread with butter.

*Potato scones are delicious served
with a hearty casserole.*

CHEESE SCONES

250 g self-raising flour
1 teaspoon baking powder
½ teaspoon dry mustard
Pinch salt
30 g butter, chilled and cubed
25 g grated parmesan cheese
90 g finely grated cheddar cheese
1 cup milk

Preheat oven to 220°C. Lightly grease a baking tray or line it with baking paper. Sift flour, baking powder, mustard and salt into a bowl. Using fingertips, rub in butter until mixture resembles fine breadcrumbs. Stir in parmesan and 60 g of the cheddar cheese, making sure they don't clump together. Make a well in the centre.

Add almost all the milk and cut in with a flat-bladed knife until dough comes together in clumps. Add some of the remaining milk if necessary. With floured hands, gently gather dough together, lift out onto a lightly floured surface and pat into a ball. Do not knead or scones will be tough.

Pat the dough out to a 2 cm thickness. Cut into 5 cm rounds. Gather the trimmings and, without over-handling, press out as before and cut more rounds. Place rounds close together on the prepared tray and sprinkle with the remaining cheese. Bake for 12–15 minutes, or until risen and golden. Serve warm.

JUNGLE SCONES

2 cups self-raising flour
1 teaspoon baking powder
30 g butter
1 egg
⅔ cup cold milk
⅓ cup hot water
½ teaspoon salt
1½ tablespoons grated cheese
1 tablespoon grated parmesan cheese
½ cup chopped parsley
¼ cup chopped chives
¼ cup other green herbs (such as mint, basil, rosemary)
Pinch mustard powder
Grated cheese, extra (optional)

Sift flour and baking powder. Rub in butter with fingertips until mixture is fine and crumbly. Reserve ½ cup of this mixture. Beat egg, milk, water and salt together. Add all other ingredients. Combine with 1½ cups flour mixture, stir vigorously, then add the reserved ½ cup flour mixture. There is no need to roll out scones; simply drop soupspoon-sized pieces onto a cold greased baking tray. Sprinkle with a little grated cheese. Bake in a hot oven for 10–12 minutes. Makes 12–14 scones.

PUMPKIN SCONES

1 tablespoon butter
1 cup caster sugar
1 cup mashed pumpkin
1 egg
3 cups self-raising flour

Beat butter and sugar to a cream, then add the mashed pumpkin
and egg. Stir in flour. If too stiff, add a little milk. Turn onto a board,
roll out and cut into desired shapes. Place on a greased tray and
bake in a hot oven for 15–20 minutes.

SULTANA SCONE SLICE

2½ cups self-raising flour
¼ cup icing sugar
1 teaspoon cinnamon, plus extra for sprinkling
Pinch salt
60 g butter, chilled and cubed
½ cup sultanas
1 egg, lightly beaten
¼ cup milk
Coffee sugar crystals

Sift flour, icing sugar, cinnamon and salt into a bowl. Rub butter into
mixture. Add sultanas. Combine beaten egg and milk, then mix into
dry ingredients. Press into a small well-greased slice tin or 18 cm
square cake tin. Sprinkle top with coffee sugar crystals and extra
cinnamon, if desired. Bake in a hot oven for 15 minutes. Allow to cool
before cutting.

VARIATION: Add 1 teaspoon ginger and 1 teaspoon mixed spice.

CHEESE BISCUITS

120 g butter, softened
90 g cheddar cheese, grated
½ teaspoon salt
¼ teaspoon cayenne pepper
1 cup self-raising flour, sifted
1 cup crushed cornflakes (about 70 g)
1 egg
1 tablespoon milk

Cream butter until soft. Add cheese, salt, cayenne, sifted flour and cornflakes. Combine egg with milk. Reserve 2 teaspoons of this mixture for glazing. Add remaining egg mixture, mix and roll teaspoonfuls of mixture into balls. Place 5 cm apart on a greased tray, press with the back of a fork, then bake in a moderate oven for 8–10 minutes. Makes 24.

BURNT BUTTER BISCUITS

125 g butter
125 g caster sugar
½ teaspoon vanilla
1 egg
185 g self-raising flour, sifted
Blanched almonds, to decorate

Place butter or margarine in a saucepan and heat until light brown in colour. Do not burn. Allow to cool. Cream melted butter and sugar. Add vanilla and egg, then flour, combining well. Roll small portions of the mixture into balls and place a blanched almond in the centre of each one. Place on a greased tray and bake in a moderate oven for 10–12 minutes.

GINGER CREAMS

250 g butter, softened
250 g caster sugar
1 egg
1 tablespoon golden syrup
2½ cups plain flour
1 teaspoon bicarbonate of soda
Pinch salt
1 tablespoon ground ginger
Plain icing

Cream butter and sugar, add egg and golden syrup and beat. Sift in dry ingredients and mix well. Drop spoonfuls of the mixture onto a greased tray and bake in a moderate oven for 15–20 minutes. When cool, ice flat side of half of biscuits, then sandwich together with remaining biscuits.

JAM DROPS

125 g butter, softened
½ cup caster sugar
1 egg
1 teaspoon vanilla
½ teaspoon salt
1½ cups self-raising flour, sifted
Raspberry jam

Cream butter and sugar to a light consistency. Add egg, vanilla and salt then beat again until blended. Fold in sifted flour. Form into walnut-sized balls and place on a greased oven tray. Make an indentation in the centre and place a small quantity of jam in each. Bake in a moderately low oven for 15 minutes.

IRENE'S BROWN CRUNCHIES

140 g plain flour
1 teaspoon baking powder
125 g butter, softened
140 g caster sugar
1 egg
1 teaspoon vanilla
1 teaspoon honey
1 teaspoon bicarbonate of soda
1½ cups rolled oats
70 g desiccated coconut
Hot water

Sift flour with baking powder. Cream butter and sugar. Add egg, vanilla, honey, bicarbonate of soda, rolled oats and coconut to creamed mixture. Add flour, then sufficient hot water to make a dough (about 1 tablespoon). Roll into balls and place on a greased tray. Press balls with a fork to flatten slightly. Bake at 150°C for 30 minutes.

ORANGE BISCUITS

125 g butter, softened
½ cup caster sugar
1 egg, beaten
Grated zest of 1 orange
1 cup self-raising flour, sifted
1 cup desiccated coconut
1 cup rolled oats

Cream butter and sugar. Add egg, zest, flour, coconut and rolled oats, mixing well. Shape teaspoonfuls of mixture into rounds and place on a greased baking tray. Bake in a moderately hot oven for 10–12 minutes.

SHEARERS' CAKES

4 cups self-raising flour
1 teaspoon cinnamon
1 teaspoon ground ginger
1 teaspoon mixed spice
1 cup caster sugar
1 cup sultanas
125 g butter, melted
2 tablespoons golden syrup
2 eggs, lightly beaten

Sift flour and spices into a bowl. Add sugar and sultanas. Combine melted butter, syrup and eggs. Add to dry ingredients. If too dry, add a little milk to make a kneading consistency. Knead well and press to a 1 cm thickness. Cut into rounds or shapes, place on a greased baking tray and bake in a moderate oven for 15 minutes or until cooked.

ANZAC BISCUITS

1 cup plain flour
⅔ cup caster sugar
1 cup rolled oats
1 cup desiccated coconut
125 g unsalted butter
¼ cup golden syrup
½ teaspoon bicarbonate of soda
1 tablespoon boiling water

Sift flour and sugar into a bowl. Add oats and coconut; make a well in the centre. Combine butter and golden syrup in a small saucepan. Stir over low heat until butter has melted and mixture is smooth; remove from heat. Dissolve bicarbonate of soda in boiling water; add immediately to butter mixture. Add butter mixture to dry ingredients. Using a wooden spoon, stir until well combined.

Drop one level tablespoon of mixture at a time onto a greased and lined 32 x 28 cm biscuit tray. Flatten gently, allowing room for spreading. Bake in a moderate oven for 20 minutes or until just browned. Remove from oven and transfer to a wire rack to cool.

SHORTBREAD

250 g butter, softened
¼ cup caster sugar
½ teaspoon vanilla
2 cups plain flour, sifted

Cream butter and sugar until light and fluffy. Mix in vanilla. Stir in sifted flour. Roll into balls, place on a greased tray and flatten with a fork. Bake in moderate oven for 12–15 minutes, or until pale golden.

APPLE SLICE

BASE
125 g butter, softened
½ cup caster sugar
1 egg
1½ cups self-raising flour, sifted

FILLING
4 medium apples
2 teaspoons lemon juice
½ cup caster sugar
¼ teaspoon ground cloves
½ teaspoon cinnamon
Passionfruit icing

To make base, cream butter and sugar, then add egg. Fold in sifted flour. Press half of the mixture into a small slice tin. Roll out the second half, ready to cover filling.

To make filling, peel and core apples, slice and cook in ½ cup water and lemon juice until tender. Drain and mash roughly, then add sugar, cloves and cinnamon. While mixture is still hot, spoon over base. Cover with the second layer of pastry and bake in a moderate oven for 25 minutes or until cooked. When cool, top with passionfruit icing.

One or more of the apples can be replaced with chokos.

APRICOT GINGER FINGERS

90 g dried apricots
1½ cups self-raising flour
1½ tablespoons cocoa
Pinch salt
¼ teaspoon cinnamon
125 g butter, chilled and cubed
¾ cup caster sugar
60 g chopped pecan nuts
90 g chopped crystallised ginger
1 egg, beaten
1 cup milk
Lemon icing (see page 102)

Soak apricots in just enough boiling water to cover the fruit. Leave for 30 minutes, until soft but not pulpy. Drain off any excess liquid (see Note).

Sift flour, cocoa, salt and cinnamon. Rub in butter, then add sugar, nuts, ginger and chopped apricots. Mix well. Fold in egg and milk. Spread into a greased and lined 25 x 30 cm Swiss roll tin. Bake in a moderate oven for 25–30 minutes. Allow to cool, then top with lemon icing. Cut into finger lengths when icing is set.

NOTE: Strained juice from apricots may be used instead of milk.

PASSIONFRUIT SLICE

BASE
125 g butter or margarine, softened
½ cup caster sugar
1 egg
1½ cups self-raising flour, sifted

TOPPING
400 g tin sweetened condensed milk
225 g tin reduced cream
½ cup lemon juice (2 lemons)
3 rounded tablespoons custard powder (90 g)
1 cup caster sugar
3 passionfruit

To make base, cream butter and sugar, add well-beaten egg, fold in sifted flour and press mixture into a greased and lined 20 x 30 cm lamington tin. Bake at 180°C for 15 minutes or until golden brown. Allow to cool.

To make topping, combine sweetened condensed milk, reduced cream and lemon juice. Spread over base. Blend custard powder, sugar and 2 cups water and boil for 5 minutes or until thickened, stirring constantly. Add passionfruit pulp, pour over filling and chill.

CARAMEL SLICE

BASE
1 cup self-raising flour, sifted
1 cup brown sugar
1 cup desiccated coconut
125 g butter, melted

FILLING
400 g tin sweetened condensed milk
60 g butter
2 tablespoons golden syrup
½ teaspoon gelatine
2 tablespoons boiling water

TOPPING
60 g butter
1 tablespoon golden syrup
1 cup desiccated coconut
½ cup rolled oats

To make base, combine flour, sugar, coconut and butter, mix well and press into a greased and lined 18 x 28 cm slice tin. Bake in a moderate oven for 20–25 minutes or until light golden. Cool slightly.

To make filling, heat condensed milk, butter and golden syrup in a saucepan until all ingredients are melted, stirring to combine. Stir through gelatine dissolved in boiling water. Stir continuously over medium heat for 10–15 minutes until caramel-brown. Cool slightly. Spread filling over base.

To make topping, melt together butter and golden syrup, then stir in coconut and oats. Mix well. Sprinkle over filling. Bake in a moderate oven for 15–20 minutes, until golden brown. Cool in tin, then cut into small squares. Not suitable for freezing.

CHERRY AND WALNUT SLICE

BASE

2 large tablespoons butter, softened
¼ cup brown sugar
1 heaped cup self-raising flour, sifted

TOPPING

2 eggs
1¼ cups brown sugar
4 tablespoons flour
1 teaspoon baking powder
½ cup drained pitted black cherries
½ cup walnuts
1 cup desiccated coconut

To make base, combine butter, sugar and flour and press into a greased and lined 18 x 26 cm slice tin. Bake in a moderate oven for 8 minutes.

To make topping, beat eggs and brown sugar. Add remaining ingredients. Spread over partly cooked base and return to oven for 20–25 minutes or until firm and golden. Mark into squares while still warm.

CHOCOLATE PEPPERMINT SLICE

BASE

125 g butter
2 tablespoons cocoa
2 eggs, beaten
1 cup caster sugar
1 cup plain flour, sifted
½ teaspoon baking powder
Pinch salt
¾ cup sultanas
1 teaspoon vanilla

TOPPING

2 tablespoons butter
1 cup icing sugar, sifted
1 tablespoon cream
½ teaspoon peppermint essence
125 g dark chocolate, melted

To make base, gently melt butter with cocoa, stirring to combine. Beat the eggs and sugar, and fold in cooled cocoa mixture. Combine with sifted flour, baking powder and salt, then add sultanas and vanilla. Pour mixture into a greased and lined 18 x 30 cm slice tin. Bake in a moderate oven for 20–25 minutes. Allow to cool.

To make topping, beat butter, icing sugar and cream together, then add peppermint essence. Spread over base, then top with melted chocolate.

VARIATION: Add 1 cup chopped walnuts to the base and, for the topping, omit peppermint and add 1 teaspoon vanilla.

CHOCOLATE ROUGH SLICE

BASE
140 g self-raising flour
Pinch salt
2 teaspoons cocoa
125 g caster sugar
40 g desiccated coconut
125 g butter, melted

TOPPING
½ cup sweetened condensed milk
1 cup icing sugar, sifted
1 cup desiccated coconut
1 tablespoon cocoa
1 teaspoon vanilla
35 g butter, melted

To make base, sift flour, salt and cocoa together, add sugar and coconut, then stir in melted butter. Mix well and press into an 18 x 26 cm slice tin. Bake in a moderate oven for 25 minutes.

To make topping, combine all ingredients over medium heat, stirring, until well mixed. Pour over base while still warm. Smooth top with a spatula dipped in hot water. Allow topping to set, then cut into slices.

COFFEE SLICE

BASE
125 g butter, softened
55 g caster sugar
150 g plain flour, sifted
40 g self-raising flour, sifted

FILLING
400 g tin sweetened condensed milk
30 g butter
2 tablespoons golden syrup
3 teaspoons instant coffee powder
40 g finely chopped walnuts

TOPPING
150 g plain flour
2 teaspoons cinnamon
55 g brown sugar (firmly packed)
125 g butter

For the base, cream together butter and sugar until just combined, then stir in flours. Mix to a firm dough. Press evenly over the base of a well-greased 25 x 30 cm Swiss roll tin. Bake in a moderate oven for 10 minutes, then spread with filling while still hot.

For the filling, combine condensed milk, butter, golden syrup and coffee in a saucepan, then stir over medium heat until mixture begins to bubble. Continue stirring briskly for about 3 minutes, or until mixture is thick. Stir in walnuts. Spread over the hot base.

To make topping, sift dry ingredients into a large bowl, then rub in butter. Mix to a firm dough, gather into a ball, wrap in plastic wrap and refrigerate for 30 minutes. Grate topping evenly over surface of filling and bake for a further 10–15 minutes, until firm to the touch. Cool in pan then cut into slices.

EASY FRUIT SLICE

250 g butter
1 cup brown sugar
1 cup mixed dried fruit
¼ cup chopped nuts or 1 cup fruit medley
1 egg
½ teaspoon vanilla
1½ cups self-raising flour
Pinch salt

Melt butter in saucepan, add sugar, stir and remove from heat. Add fruit and nuts, beat in egg and vanilla, then fold in flour and salt. Spread mixture in a greased and lined lamington tin and bake in a moderate oven for 20–25 minutes. When cool, cut the slice into finger lengths.

LATTICE CREAM SLICE

250 g cream cheese, softened
250 g unsalted butter, softened
1 cup caster sugar
1 dessertspoon gelatine
¼ cup boiling water
2 packets Lattice biscuits
Icing sugar

Cream together the cheese, butter and sugar. Dissolve gelatine in boiling water, add to cheese mixture and mix well. Line a Swiss roll tin with foil. Place biscuits from 1 packet on the foil, dull side facing up. Spread creamed mixture over biscuits and top with remaining packet of biscuits, shiny side up. Sift icing sugar over top to decorate. Chill until ready to serve.

GINGER FANTASY BAR

BASE
250 g butter, softened
125 g caster sugar
2 cups self-raising flour, sifted
1 teaspoon ground ginger

TOPPING
2 eggs
1¼ cups brown sugar
¾ cup raisins
¼ cup chopped nuts
¼ cup chopped glacé cherries
¼ cup chopped glacé ginger
1 cup desiccated coconut
90 g self-raising flour

To make the base, cream butter and sugar, then add sifted flour and ground ginger. Press into a greased and lined 20 x 30 cm slice tin. Bake in a moderate oven until partly cooked (about 15 minutes).

To make topping, beat eggs and sugar together until fluffy. Add all remaining ingredients and pour over the hot half-cooked base. Return to oven and bake a further 30–35 minutes, or until a skewer comes out clean. If surface is browning too quickly, cover tin with baking paper or foil.

NO-BAKE CHOCOLATE SLICE

125 g butter
125 g caster sugar
1 dessertspoon drinking chocolate
1 packet plain biscuits, crushed
1 egg
200 g fruit and nut chocolate
60 g Copha

Melt butter with the sugar, add drinking chocolate and biscuits and bring to the boil. Cool and add well-beaten egg. Press into a slice pan and place in refrigerator. Melt chocolate and Copha, then pour over the firm base. Refrigerate until set.

OLD-FASHIONED RAISIN BARS

1 cup chopped raisins
125 g butter
1 cup caster sugar
1 egg, beaten
1¾ cups plain flour
1 level teaspoon bicarbonate of soda
1 teaspoon each nutmeg, ground cloves and allspice
Pinch salt
½ cup chopped walnuts
Icing sugar, sifted, for sprinkling

Place raisins in saucepan, add 1 cup water and bring to the boil. Remove from heat and add butter. Cool until lukewarm, then stir in sugar and egg. Sift together dry ingredients and add to the mixture. Stir in walnuts. Pour into a greased and lined 20 x 30 cm baking tin and bake in a moderate oven for approximately 20 minutes. Remove from pan and cut into bars. Sprinkle with icing sugar.

OPERA HOUSE SLICE

BASE
125 g butter, melted
½ cup icing sugar
1 cup plain flour, sifted

TOPPING
60 g butter
⅓ cup caster sugar
1 tablespoon milk
1 teaspoon vanilla
1½ cups mixed dried fruit
¼ cup slivered almonds

To make base, mix butter, icing sugar and sifted flour together, then press into a greased and lined 17 x 27 cm slice tin. Cook in a 180°C oven for 10–12 minutes until brown and cooked through.

To make topping, melt butter, then add sugar, milk, vanilla and mixed dried fruit. Heat until bubbling, then add almonds. Spread over base, then return to oven and cook for 5–10 minutes until bubbling. Cool in tin then slice into squares or fingers.

HONEYCOMB CHEESECAKE SLICE

BASE
¾ cup self-raising flour
⅓ cup brown sugar
⅓ cup desiccated coconut
1 tablespoon cocoa
90 g butter, melted

TOPPING
500 g cream cheese
⅓ cup caster sugar
½ cup sour cream
2 teaspoons gelatine
1½ tablespoons hot water
100 g chocolate coated honeycomb bars or pieces

Preheat the oven to 180°C. Spray a 30 x 20 cm slice tin with non-stick cooking spray. For the base, mix ingredients until combined. Press mixture into the prepared tin and bake for 15–20 minutes. Remove from oven and allow to cool.

In a bowl, beat the cream cheese, sugar and sour cream together until smooth. Dissove gelatine in hot water and beat into the cheese mixture. Roughly chop the honeycomb and fold into the mixture. Pour over the cooled base and leave to set in refrigerator.

LEMON SLICE

SHORTBREAD BASE
125 g butter or margarine, softened
125 g caster sugar
1 egg
250 g plain flour

LEMON FILLING
1 cup sugar
Grated zest and juice of 3 lemons
½ cup cornflour, blended with ⅓ cup cold water

CREAM TOPPING
1½ cups milk
1½ tablespoons caster sugar
1½ tablespoons cornflour
1 teaspoon butter
1 teaspoon vanilla
¼ cup desiccated coconut

For the base, cream butter and sugar, add egg and mix well. Add flour and mix to a stiff dough. Press into base of lightly greased shallow tin. Bake in a moderate oven for 20–25 minutes.

For filling, place sugar, lemon juice, zest and 1¼ cups water in a saucepan. Bring to the boil. Thicken with blended cornflour. Cook for 1 minute, stirring constantly. Cool slightly. Pour over base and chill until firm.

For the cream topping, heat milk and sugar together, stir in cornflour blended with 3 tablespoons of water. Cook until thickened, stirring constantly. Add butter and vanilla. Stir until butter has melted. Pour over lemon layer. Sprinkle with coconut. Allow to cool then cut into squares.

COCONUT DELIGHT

1 cup self-raising flour
1 tablespoon cocoa
1 cup cornflakes
½ cup caster sugar
1 cup desiccated coconut, plus extra for decoration
⅔ cup butter
1 dessertspoon golden syrup
½ teaspoon vanilla
Chocolate icing

Sift flour and cocoa. Add cornflakes, sugar and coconut. Melt butter, golden syrup and vanilla and mix into dry ingredients. Press into a greased and lined 17 x 26 cm tray and bake in a moderate oven for 20–25 minutes. When cold, top with chocolate icing and sprinkle with coconut.

CHOCOLATE MARSHMALLOW SLICE

200 g marshmallows
60 g butter
125 g dark chocolate, chopped
1 teaspoon vanilla
125 g walnuts, chopped
Brandy or rum, optional

Place marshmallows, butter and 1 tablespoon water in the microwave for 2 minutes on medium–high. Remove, then stir in chocolate and vanilla until chocolate has melted. Beat until smooth and creamy, then add nuts and brandy or rum, if using. Spread in a greased and lined bar tin and refrigerate overnight. Cut into small squares.

CASHEW BROWNIES

200 g chopped dark chocolate
175 g butter, chopped
2 eggs
1 cup soft brown sugar
1 cup plain flour
⅓ cup cocoa
½ cup unsalted cashews, toasted and chopped
100 g chopped dark chocolate, extra

ICING
200 g chopped dark chocolate
½ cup sour cream
¼ cup icing sugar

Preheat oven to 160°C. Lightly grease a 23 cm square shallow tin and line base with baking paper.

Melt dark chocolate and butter in a heatproof bowl over (not touching) simmering water, stirring to combine. Allow to cool.

Whisk eggs and soft brown sugar in a large bowl for 5 minutes, or until pale and thick. Fold in cooled chocolate mixture, then sifted flour and cocoa. Fold in cashews and extra chocolate, then pour into tin, smoothing the top. Bake for 30–35 minutes, or until just firm to the touch; do not overcook. (The brownies may have a slightly soft centre when hot but will firm when cool.) Allow to cool.

For the icing, melt chocolate in a small heatproof bowl over (not touching) simmering water, stirring frequently. Allow to cool slightly, then add sour cream and icing sugar and mix well. Spread evenly over cooled brownies. Leave for a few hours or overnight to firm, then cut into squares.

Store in an airtight container for up to 5 days, or freeze for up to 3 months.

MUESLI SLICE

250 g butter, diced
2 tablespoons honey
1 cup caster sugar
2½ cups rolled oats
¾ cup desiccated coconut
1 cup cornflakes, lightly crushed
½ cup flaked almonds
1 teaspoon ground mixed spice
45 g finely chopped dried apricots
1 cup dried mixed fruit

Preheat oven to 160°C. Grease a 20 x 30 cm tin and line with baking paper, leaving paper hanging over two long sides.

Combine butter, honey and sugar in a small saucepan and stir over low heat for 5 minutes, or until butter has melted and caster sugar has dissolved.

Mix remaining ingredients together in a bowl and make a well in the centre. Pour in butter mixture and stir well, then press into the tin. Bake for 45 minutes or until golden. Cool completely in the tin, then refrigerate for 2 hours or until firm.

Lift slice from tin using paper as handles. Cut into pieces. Store in an airtight container for up to 3 days. Makes 18.

MARSHMALLOW BARS

BASE
125 g butter
2½ tablespoons cocoa
½ cup caster sugar
1 egg, beaten
1¼ teaspoons vanilla
¾ cup sultanas
1 cup desiccated coconut
1½ cups wheatmeal biscuit crumbs

TOPPING
4½ tablespoons gelatine
4 cups caster sugar
1 teaspoon vanilla
1 tablespoon lemon juice
Pink food colouring (optional)

For the base, melt butter, cocoa and sugar and boil until sugar is dissolved. Remove from heat, cool then add egg and vanilla. Stir in sultanas, coconut and biscuit crumbs and mix well. Press into a greased and lined 20 x 30 cm lamington tray. Chill in refrigerator.

For topping, add gelatine to 1 cup cold water and let stand for 5 minutes. Combine sugar and 1½ cups water in a large saucepan and stir constantly over medium heat until sugar is dissolved. Add the gelatine and boil for 20 minutes longer. Allow to cool then add vanilla, lemon juice and colouring, if using, and beat until stiff. Pour over base and chill until set. Cut slice into bars.

NITA'S DATE SLICE

2 cups self-raising flour, sifted
1 cup brown sugar
145 g butter, chilled and cubed
1 egg
1 cup milk
1 teaspoon baking powder
1 cup chopped dates

ICING
1½ cups icing sugar
10 g butter, softened
2 tablespoons milk
¼ teaspoon coffee essence

Preheat oven to 180°C. Grease and flour a 17 x 27 cm slice tin.
Place the flour and brown sugar in mixing bowl. Rub in butter with
fingertips until well combined and crumbly. Place half of this dry
mixture into a greased and lined slice tin, pressing down firmly.

Mix together egg, milk and baking powder. Add chopped dates,
stir to combine and add all of this mixture into second half of mixture
in bowl. Pour over base mixture in tin. Bake in preheated oven for
30–40 minutes.

For the icing, combine all ingredients until smooth. When the
slice is cold, ice and cut into 24 pieces.

NOTE: The slice freezes well, but is more presentable if you ice it
after thawing. You can also substitute any dried fruit for the dates.

INDEX

Published in 2018 by Murdoch Books, an imprint of Allen & Unwin

Murdoch Books Australia
83 Alexander Street
Crows Nest NSW 2065
Phone: +61 (0) 2 8425 0100
Fax: +61 (0) 2 9906 2218
murdochbooks.com.au
info@murdochbooks.com.au

Murdoch Books UK
Ormond House
26–27 Boswell Street
London WC1N 3JZ
Phone: +44 (0) 20 8785 5995
murdochbooks.co.uk
info@murdochbooks.co.uk

For Corporate Orders & Custom Publishing,
contact our Business Development Team at
salesenquiries@murdochbooks.com.au

Publisher: Corinne Roberts
Design Manager: Vivien Valk
Layout: transformer.com.au
Editor: Janine Flew
Food Editor: Grace Campbell
Food Consultant: Pauline Hunt
Production Director: Lou Playfair

PLEASE NOTE: The recipes in this book were previously published in
The Country Women's Association Cookbook 2, first published 2011.

Text © 2011 and 2018 Murdoch Books/Country Women's Association of NSW
The moral rights of the author have been asserted.
Design © Murdoch Books 2018

All rights reserved. No part of this publication may be reproduced, stored in a
retrieval system or transmitted in any form or by any means, electronic, mechanical,
photocopying, recording or otherwise, without the prior written permission of the
publisher.

A cataloguing-in-publication entry is available from the catalogue of the National
Library of Australia at nla.gov.au.

ISBN 978 1 76052 366 4

Printed by C&C Offset Printing Co, Ltd, China
10 9 8 7 6 5

IMPORTANT: Those who might be at risk from the effects of salmonella poisoning
(the elderly, pregnant women, young children and those suffering from immune
deficiency diseases) should consult their doctor with concerns about eating raw eggs.

OVEN GUIDE: You may find cooking times vary depending on the oven you are
using. For fan-forced ovens, as a general rule, set the oven temperature to 20°C
(70°F) lower than indicated in the recipe.

MEASURES GUIDE: We have used 20 ml (4 teaspoon) tablespoon measures. If you
are using a 15 ml (3 teaspoon) tablespoon add an extra teaspoon of the ingredient for
each tablespoon specified.

MIX
Paper | Supporting
responsible forestry
FSC® C008047
FSC
www.fsc.org